LOCOMOTIVES

in detail

MAUNSELL 4-4-0 **6** SCHOOLS CLASS

LOCOMOTIVES
in detail
6

MAUNSELL 4-4-0　　　　**SCHOOLS CLASS**

PETER SWIFT

Ian Allan PUBLISHING

This is the third in this series of books to deal with locomotives of the Southern Railway. It is intended to provide modellers with detailed information on the appearance of the locomotives described, at each period of their history.

When I was growing up in Winchester in the late 1940s and 1950s, the 'Schools' were the unknowns amongst the Southern's express classes. Some had been allocated to Bournemouth in the late 1930s but during the 1950s, they were all on the Eastern section, with only periodic visits to Eastleigh Works to bring them to Hampshire. One day in 1957, I came onto the up platform at Winchester to catch a train to London. In the down platform was a strange flat sided six-car multiple-unit train. Multiple-units encountered in the London area were totally silent whilst standing still, producing only a subdued whine when they moved off. This one was thumping and twittering at both ends! Although I did not know it at the time, the presence of this unit, presumably on a trial run from Eastleigh, was the sign of the coming return of 'Schools' class locomotives to the Bournemouth line. The 'Schools' were displaced from the Hastings line by diesel electric multiple-units of the type which I had seen and, a few years later, were displaced from the Kent Coast main lines by electrification

Numerous books and articles have been published describing various aspects of the Maunsell 'Schools' class 4-4-0s of the Southern Railway. Those which have been of most use in preparing the text for this book are listed in the bibliography, in the order of publication. For additional information, I am indebted to the staff at the National Railway Museum and the National Archive, who made available maintenance records. Keith Gays provided information on No. 30926 on the North Yorkshire Moors Railway and John Davis confirmed the connection between the J. Stones speedometer on No. 939 and the later British Railways equipment.

For the provision of photographs, I am indebted to all those photographers whose material has found its way into my own collection over many years, in many cases with no record of the source of the photograph. Alan Butcher of the Ian Allan organisation allowed me free access to the Ian Allan photographic archive and Mike King has supplied prints from the Ted West collection, which he holds on behalf of the South Western Circle. Rod Blencowe and Brian Stephenson have also supplied prints from their collections to fill some of the gaps in the pictorial story of the 'Schools'.

The late George Woodward kept a week by week record of everything which came into Eastleigh Works from 1926 to the 1960s. Without his notes, all subsequent writers would have been left guessing about many aspects of what happened, particularly regarding liveries, that most contentious of issues with modellers. I am also most grateful to Eric Youldon and John Harvey who have long been researching the details of Southern locomotives. Both of these gentlemen looked through my draft texts and suggested many amendments, additions and corrections. My draft tables, when sent to them for their comments, contained many gaps and guesses. They returned the comprehensive set of data which you will find at the end of the book. However, new photographs still keep appearing which alter the accepted dates of minor changes.

Peter H. Swift, Spondon, Derby March 2006

Bibliography
S. C. Townroe, *The Book of the Schools Class*, Ian Allan 1949.
H. Holcroft, *Locomotive Adventure Volume 1*, Ian Allan 1962.
H. Holcroft, *Locomotive Adventure Volume 2*, Ian Allan 1965.
L. Tavender, *Livery Register No. 3 LSWR and Southern*, HMRS 1970.
S. C. Townroe, *The Arthurs, Nelsons and Schools of the Southern*, Ian Allan, 1973.
D. L. Bradley, *Locomotives of the Southern Railway, Part 1*, RCTS, 1975.
S. C. Townroe, *Arthurs, Nelsons & Schools at Work*, Ian Allan, 1982.
B. Haresnape, *Railway Liveries - Southern Railway*, Ian Allan, 1982.
J. E. Chacksfield, *Richard Maunsell An Engineering Biography*, Oakwood, 1998.

Series Created & Edited by Jasper Spencer-Smith.
Design and artwork: Nigel Pell.
Produced by JSS Publishing Limited, P.O. Box 6031, Bournemouth, Dorset, England.

Title spread: No. 30926 *Repton* prepared for a Royal Train working at Stewarts Lane in June 1962. (CR/JWFP)

First published 2006

ISBN (10) 0 7110 3178 9
ISBN (13) 0 7110 3178 4

Published by Ian Allan Publishing

an imprint of Ian Allan Publishing Ltd, Hersham, Surrey KT12 4RG.
Printed in England by Ian Allan Printing Ltd, Hersham, Surrey KT12 4RG.

Code: 06011/B2

Visit the Ian Allan Publishing website at www.ianallanpublishing.com

Photograph Credits
Colour-Rail (CR) and their photographers
Pendragon Collection (PC); R. H. N. Hardy (RHNH); J. Kinnison (JK);
H. M. Lane (HML); J. W. Millibank (JWM); J. W. F. Paige (JWFP);
N. Sprinks (NS); A. Trickett (AT); S. C. Townroe (ST).
R. K. Blencowe/Transport Treasury (RKB)
A. C. Causton (ACC); A. W. Croughton (AWC); E. W. Fry (EWF);
W. Gilburt (WG); L. G. Marshall (LGM); P. Winding (PW).
Rail Archives Stephenson (RAS)
C. R. L. Coles (CRLC); R. S. Clark (RSC); G. R. Griggs (GRG);
O. J. Morris (OJM); B. Whicher (BW); J. P. Wilson (JPW).
Ian Allan Library (IA)
A. R. Butcher (ARB); C. P. Boocock (CPB); N. Brayshaw (NB); R. W. Beaton (RWB); A. G. Coombs (AGC); B. K. Cooper (BKC); D. B. Clark (DBC); D. Cross (DC); M. W. Earley (MWE); M. J. Fox (MJF); F. F. Moss (FFM); D. C. Oveden (DCO); J. W. F. Paige (JFWP); R. A. Panting (RAP); J. G. Reynolds (JGR); R. C. Riley (RCR); R. Russell (RR); A. A. Sellman; (AAS); J. Scrace (JS); Eric Treacy (ET); E. R. Wethersett (ERW); G. Wheeler (GW); P. Ransome Wallis (PRW).
R. S. Carpenter Colection (RSC)
H. F. Wheeler (HFW).
Others
D. L. Bradley (DLB); H. C. Casserley (HCC); Stephenson Locomotive Society (SLS); R. F. Roberts (RFB); B. Whicher (BW); A. E. West/South Western Circle (AEW/SWC); Authors Collection (AC).

INTRODUCTION

The Maunsell 'Schools' class locomotives were built to
work the secondary express trains of the Southern Railway,
over main lines which could accept high axle loading.

Compared with the 'Merchant Navy' Pacifics, described by John Harvey in No. 1 of this series of books, and the 'King Arthur' 4-6-0s, described by the present author in No. 4, the 'Schools' class 4-4-0s are simplicity itself; 40 locomotives built over a six year period in the Southern Railway's works at Eastleigh, Hampshire. There were few variations between the members of the class and few of the modifications which were carried out resulted in their appearance being changed greatly. The lack of variation, either in build standard or by modification, is itself a statement that the 'Schools' class 4-4-0s were 'right straight out of the box'.

THE REQUIREMENT

At the end of the 1920s, the Southern Railway had 74 two-cylinder express passenger 4-6-0s of the 'King Arthur' class and 16 larger four-cylinder 4-6-0s of the 'Lord Nelson' class, for the heaviest work. Fifty-five of the 4-6-0s were based on the Western section, 14 on the Central section and 21 on the Eastern section. These were supported by numerous older express locomotives from the three constituents of the Southern Railway. On the Eastern section, the 4-6-0s were used primarily on the boat trains from London to Dover and Folkestone. The majority of other expresses were in the hands of the 30 'D1' and 'E1'

class 4-4-0s, rebuilt between 1919 and 1927 from locomotives of the old South Eastern and Chatham Railways, with superheated boilers and long travel valves. There were also the 15 similar, but slightly larger, 'L1s' built new for the Southern Railway. These were excellent locomotives but were rather small by the standards of the day.

On the Central Section, the London, Brighton & South Coast Railway had used large tank engines for many of its expresses. When Maunsell was appointed Chief Mechanical Engineer to the South Eastern and Chatham Railways Managing Committee in 1914, he had followed this example with a two-cylinder 2-6-4T of class K, more of which were built by the Southern Railway and named after rivers in Southern England. By 1927, there were 20 of the two-cylinder 'River Class' 2-6-4Ts in service (A790-A809) and a single three-cylinder 'K1' (A890). These worked express trains on the Central and Eastern sections until, on 21 August 1927, No. A 800 *River Cray* became derailed near Sevenoaks whilst working a Cannon Street to Deal express, leading to 13 fatalities when the carriages were thrown against the abutments of an overbridge which the train was approaching at the time. At the subsequent enquiry, it became apparent that the quality of the Eastern Section's track left much to be desired and that the 'River' class, with the water carried high up alongside the boiler, were apt to roll on less than perfect track.

Above:
The 'King Arthur' class 4-6-0s were the Southern Railway's principal express locomotives in the 1920s but, out of 74 locomotives, only 10 were used on the Eastern Section, mainly on the Continental boat trains. E772 *Sir Percivale* was one of 30 built by the North British Locomotive Company in 1925. (AC)

Left:
For the heaviest duties, the Southern had 16 of Maunsell's four-cylinder 'Lord Nelson' class 4-6-0s, 11 of which were allocated to the Eastern Section for boat train duties. E851 *Sir Francis Drake* was built at the Southern's Eastleigh works in 1928. (AC)

Right:
The majority of the express passenger trains on the Eastern Section were in the hands of Maunsell's 4-4-0s of the 'D1', 'E1' and 'L1' classes. A757 was built by the North British Locomotive Company in 1926. Although excellent locomotives, they were too small for the coming requirements. (AC)

This had not been the first derailment of the class, but the others had not led to any serious consequences. A decision to rebuild the 'Rivers' into 2-6-0s with tenders was an inevitable outcome of the enquiry into the derailment. These became the first of the 'U' and 'U1' class locomotives, retaining the same numbers but without names. It is likely that the Eastern section running department was pleased with the decision as, although a tank engine was a reasonable solution to the 51-mile run from Victoria to Brighton, the 78-mile run to Dover or 79 miles to Margate were a bit far for comfort.

The Southern required a locomotive to replace the older 4-4-0s on its secondary expresses, and to run on lines where the 4-6-0s were not permitted. These included the Tonbridge-Hastings line which had a reduced loading gauge. Shortly after the line opened in the 1850s, problems were experienced in a number of tunnels on the line. On investigation, it was found that the contractor had used only a single ring of bricks for the tunnel lining, where four had been specified. The only realistic solution had been to insert additional rings of bricks inside the tunnel. The reduced loading gauge did not become a problem until the first of Maunsell's 'N' class 2-6-0s and 'K' class 2-6-4Ts appeared in 1917, and were too wide for the line. To update the motive power on the Hastings line, it was essential that the new express locomotive should comply with its loading gauge.

Right:
Following the lead given by the London, Brighton & South Coast Railway, Maunsell had introduced large-wheeled tank engines for the express services of the South Eastern & Chatham Railways, with one 2-6-4T of the 'K' class in 1917. These were followed by 20 more, now named the 'River' class, in Southern Railway days. A802 *River Cuckmere* was built at the Southern's Brighton works in 1926. Following the derailment of A800 *River Cray* near Sevenoaks in 1927 all the 'River' class were rebuilt as 'U' class 2-6-0s in 1928. (AC)

CONCEPTION OF THE SCHOOLS CLASS

One of Maunsell's assistants, Harold Holcroft, had previously been an assistant to G.J. Churchward on the Great Western Railway (GWR) at Swindon. He had produced a design for a mechanism to work the valve of the middle cylinder of a three cylinder locomotive from the two valve gears of the outside cylinders. This had not been taken up by the GWR, which used either two or four cylinders on its locomotives. Holcroft moved to the South Eastern & Chatham Railway (SE&CR) as Maunsell's personal assistant in 1914 and was employed initially on reorganising the company's Ashford (Kent) works. During a bout of sickness, he drew up a design for a three-cylinder 4-4-0 with his derived valve gear and showed this to Maunsell. The three-cylinder arrangement had three clear advantages over the conventional two-cylinder layout.

1) For a given power requirement, the cylinders could be smaller than those on a two-cylinder locomotive, reducing the width of the locomotive.
2) With six impulses per rotation of the wheels, the tractive force applied by the locomotive is more even than for a two-cylinder locomotive, with four impulses per rotation of the wheels.
3) On a two-cylinder locomotive, the cranks had to be set at 90° to each other, to ensure that at least one cylinder would always apply a turning force to the wheels to start the train. This caused unbalanced reciprocating forces due to the masses of the pistons, crossheads

and connecting rods moving backwards and forwards. These forces could only be balanced by counter-weights on the wheels or on the crank axle. However, balancing a horizontal reciprocating force by a rotating centrifugal force caused a vertical force, known as hammer blow, between the wheels and the rails. On a three-cylinder locomotive with the cranks set 120° apart the reciprocating masses would largely balance each other and the only balance weights required on the wheels were those to counter the centrifugal forces of the rotating crank and the big ends of the connecting rods. In practice, most locomotive engineers of the time provided some reciprocating balance for three cylinder locomotives.

The first and third advantages also applied to four-cylinder locomotives in which the cranks were equally spaced at 90°. The main disadvantage was that a three-cylinder or four-cylinder locomotive was heavier and more expensive to build than an equivalent two-cylinder one. There were also more components to maintain but the smoother running tended to reduce the wear and tear on the machinery. Maunsell produced a three-cylinder 2-6-0 (Class N1) with Holcroft's derived valve gear, which could run between Tonbridge and Hastings, as its outside cylinders were smaller than on the 'N' class. However, its derived valve gear required considerable maintenance and, when more 'N1s' were built in Southern days, Maunsell used a third set of Walschaerts gear for the inside cylinder.

Above:
To try out Holcroft's ideas, Maunsell built a three-cylinder version of his 2-6-0, 'N1' class, in 1923. Five more, A876 to A880, were built at Ashford in 1930, but with three sets of Walschaerts valve gear in place of the Holcroft derived valve gear. All were built to the reduced Hastings line loading gauge and ran with the same type of tender as the 'Schools' class, but without the turned in sides. The tender running plate is joggled at the front to raise it to the Ashford standard height. (IA)

CHAPTER ONE

DESIGN, CONSTRUCTION & MAINTENANCE

The Southern's requirement for a secondary express locomotive
was met by the most powerful 4-4-0 in Europe, capable
of working all but the heaviest of the company's trains.

For the new Express Locomotive, the three-cylinder arrangement had been defined by loading gauge requirements. Assuming that a front bogie would be required for good riding, the next question was whether to build a high axle load 4-4-0 or a low axle load 4-6-0. When faced with the same question a few years earlier, Gresley had built both for the LNER; a three-cylinder 4-4-0 ('D49' class) for North East England and Scotland and a three-cylinder 4-6-0 ('B17' class) for East Anglia, where the tracks could not carry a 20-ton axle load. On the lines where the SR wanted their intermediate express locomotives to run, axle load was not a problem but there were short turntables at a number of the depots where the new locomotives were to be based, which could not turn a 4-6-0. Maunsell thus chose the 4-4-0 wheel arrangement and the Southern Railway became the proud owner of 'The Most Powerful 4-4-0 in Europe'. There were bigger locomotives in the US, where 30-ton axle loads were commonplace.

DESIGN

Having reached the decision to build a three-cylinder 4-4-0, the details required to be worked out. To use as many existing compo-

nents as possible, Maunsell wanted the locomotive to be three quarters of a 'Lord Nelson' 4-6-0, with one axle and one cylinder removed, and with a derivative of the 'Lord Nelson'-type boiler and with a Belpaire firebox. An initial design was prepared, but proved to be too heavy. Additionally, the high shoulders of the Belpaire firebox would restrict the driver's view from the narrow cab, required to fit the Hastings line loading gauge. A decision was then made to use a shortened version of the 'King Arthur' boiler, with a round topped firebox. The boiler barrel was shortened by 2ft (61cm), losing the part of the tubes where steam generation was the least, as the combustion gases cooled towards the front of the boiler. The grate area was reduced from 30sqft (2.8sqm) to 28.3sqft (2.63sqm).

Following unsatisfactory experience with the Holcroft-designed conjugated valve gear on the first 'N1' class 2-6-0 and 'K1' class 2-6-4T, three sets of Walschaerts valve gear were used. The crosshead of the centre cylinder drove a vacuum pump. This was standard on the Maunsell 4-6-0s, but on these classes had been visible below the left-hand lower slidebar. The slidebars of the new locomotives were of three-bar pattern, above the piston rod. Although, theoretically, none should have been

Above:
The first of the 'Schools' classs, E900 *Eton,* in 'photographic' grey at Eastleigh in 1930. It shows the features of the first 10 of the class which were changed on later locomotives. The smokebox side-lamp irons are clearly seen. A feature unique to E900 is the lack of any handrail to assist the crew when climbing onto the front platform. (AC)

Left:
No. 910 *Merchant Taylors,* as built in December 1932. This was the first of the second batch of 'Schools' locomotives, built new with smoke deflectors, steam sanding to all driving wheels and the raised cabside windows. It still has the early bogie frame. (AC)

Above:
E901 *Winchester* as built in March 1930. The photograph shows the features of the first 10 of the class which were changed on later builds. There are no smoke deflector plates, the main frames in front of the cylinders are covered by snap head rivets and the bogie side frames have a V-shaped lower edge. There is no sanding to the rear coupled wheels and the cabside windows are set low, with no visors over the front spectacles. The tender has the toolboxes set longitudinally either side at the front. (AC)

required, balancing of 30% of the reciprocating masses was provided. The 'Schools' class were built to an overall width of 8ft 6in (2.59m) to fit the restricted Hastings line loading gauge. The upper part of the cabside was angled inwards to clear the curve of the tunnel sides and the tender coping was angled in to match the cab.

In 1925, the SR Public Relations Officer John Elliot had recommended that the Company's express locomotives should carry names. Following the 'King Arthur' and 'Lord Nelson' 4-6-0s and the 'River' 2-6-4Ts, it was inevitable that the new 4-4-0s would be named. Names of counties or cities were considered but the Great Western Railway already had both of these and the Southern system did not serve enough of either for the projected number of locomotives, so the names of public schools were chosen. Following the classification practice of the South Eastern & Chatham Railways, the new 4-4-0s were identified as Class 'V' but were always better known as the 'Schools' class. Unlike Maunsell's 'Lord Nelsons', where the 'most powerful' claim was quickly challenged by the other three British railway companies, there was no challenge to the Southern's 4-4-0, although the Great Northern Railway of Ireland's (GNR[I]) class 'V' compound 4-4-0s of 1932

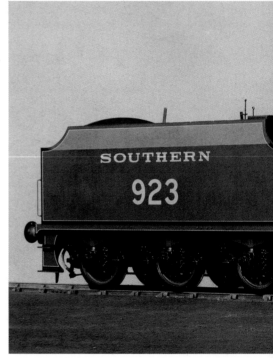

and the Class 'VS' three-cylinder simples of 1948 came close. It must have been a coincidence that the SR and the GNR(I), both of which used letter classifications for locomotives, arrived at 'V' at around the same time, and with similar locomotives.

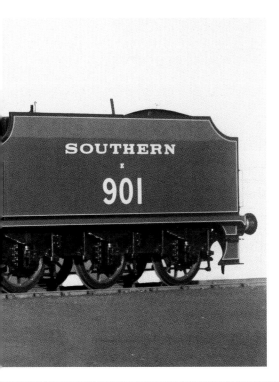

were numbered E900 to E909, the E-prefix identifying that the overhaul workshop was Eastleigh. Twenty more, with some modifications, were built to order No. E403 between December 1932 and July 1934. The modifications are described in detail in chapter 3. By this date, the Southern had stopped using letter prefixes and the locomotives carried the Numbers 910 to 929. A final 10 locomotives, Nos. 930 to 939, were built to order No. E496 between December 1934 and July 1935.

MAINTENANCE

Maintenance might seem irrelevant in a book dealing primarily with the external appearance of locomotives, but an understanding of maintenance procedures does explain why and when many changes to the appearance of the locomotives occurred. The locomotives were originally scheduled to receive a Class A overhaul, reclassified as a General Overhaul in

Below:
No. 923 *Uppingham* as built in December 1933, showing the features of the later locomotives. Smoke deflector plates are fitted, the main frames in front of the cylinders are assembled using countersunk rivets and the later type of bogie side frame, with a straight lower edge, is fitted. There is now steam sanding to all driving wheels and the cab has the side windows raised and visors over the front spectacles. The tender has transverse toolboxes. (AC)

CONSTRUCTION

The first ten of the 'Schools' class 4-4-0s were built at the company's works at Eastleigh, Hampshire, to order No. E378. They were completed between March and July 1930 and

British Railways (BR) days, every 70,000 miles (112,651km). This was increased to 85,000 miles (136,790km) by Bulleid and was frequently exceeded, particularly during the war years and in BR days. Class A overhauls occurred approximately every two years and

took around a month. At the overhaul, the locomotive would be lifted off its wheels, worn or damaged components brought back to standard and modifications carried out. The boiler might be changed and the overhaul would be finished with a full repaint in the current livery. There were 45 boilers, numbered 807 to 816 and 1007 to 1041, for the 40 locomotives. As there were no visible differences between them there will be no further reference to boiler exchanges.

Class B (Intermediate) overhauls were carried out at approximately the halfway stage between Class As. Locomotives might also visit the main workshops for Class C (unclassified) repairs. These would occur due to accident damage or other defects which were beyond the capability of the running sheds. Intermediate or unclassified repairs might be completed by touching up the paintwork or renumbering. Although nominally allocated to Eastleigh for overhaul until 1956, there were a number of instances when 'Schools' went to other SR workshops at Ashford, Kent, or Brighton, Sussex, for overhaul. Bricklayers Arms shed in South London also had a heavy repair shop which could, and did, cope with any maintenance short of a full class A or General Overhaul.

No. 30902 *Wellington* in the erecting shop at Ashford works, towards the end of a General Overhaul, 4 May 1959. The cab floor is missing, but will be boarded over to the level of the raised running plate. AWS equipment has been fitted during the overhaul. (IA/RB)

No. 928 *Stowe* at Bournemouth shed, 19 July 1937. Not every locomotive always ran perfectly; even the 'Schools' had occasional problems. No. 928 appears to have run a hot axlebox on the trailing coupled axle and has been lifted on the shearlegs at the shed. With the open-sided lifting road directly opposite the extended down platform of Bournemouth Central station, this was a very public location to show a defect. (HCC)

CHAPTER TWO

MAUNSELL MODIFICATIONS

A number of modifications were designed
and fitted to the 'Schools' class as successive
batches of locomotives were built.

As the 'Schools'-class locomotives were a success from the start, there was no need to carry out many modifications to improve performance. There were a number of minor problems with the first 10 locomotives, which were corrected in the last 30 locomotives built and, in some cases, applied retrospectively to the first 10. Other modifications were applied later to some locomotives, but few gave enough of an improvement to justify fitting to the entire class. Where known, the dates at which these modifications were applied are shown in the Appendix.

SMOKE DEFLECTORS

The first 10 locomotives were built without smoke deflectors, at first sight a surprising omission. Smoke deflector plates had proved necessary on the 'King Arthur' class, to prevent the exhaust from blowing down over the boiler and obscuring the driver's view up the line. After a number of trials, a satisfactory design had been produced and was fitted to all the 'King Arthur' and 'Lord Nelson' 4-6-0s by 1929. However, the 'King Arthur'-type deflectors had not totally solved the problems. At the time the first 'Schools' were being built, wind tunnel tests were being carried out at the National Physical Laboratory on a scale model

of a 'Schools' locomotive, to develop a more effective smoke deflector plate.

The tests resulted in deflector plates which were extended forward, compared with those on the 'King Arthur' class, and were mounted vertically, instead of being angled inwards. These changes enabled the plates to collect more clean air at the front of the locomotive, to lift the exhaust and to provide a flow of clean air along the side of the boiler. 'Schools' class locomotives Nos. 910 to 939 were built with these modified deflector plates and Nos. E900 to E909 were provided with them at the first overhaul.

CHIMNEYS

Nos. 915 *Brighton* and 916 *Whitgift* were built and fitted with a chimney without a capuchon. Similar chimneys appeared from time to time on other 'Schools' locomotives, such as No. 901 *Winchester* in the mid-1930s.

LAMP IRON AND FRONT HANDRAILS

On the first 10 locomotives, the lamp irons to either side of the smokebox were mounted on the edge of the smokebox. A route disc on one of these would have been in the driver's line of sight, so these lamp irons were moved onto the

Above:
E901 *Winchester* passing Chelsfield on a Charing Cross to Deal express in 1931. Lamp irons are now on the smokebox door and sanding has been provided to the rear coupled wheels. The LSWR-style gilt sans serif buffer beam numerals were carried when new by E900 and E901 only. (AC)

Left:
No. 909 *St Pauls* in the early 1930s. It has received smoke deflector plates, steam sanding to all driving wheels and the smoke-box lamp irons are now on the door. It also has the later pattern bogie frames, with a straight lower edge. The cab still has no visors over the front spectacles. (RAS)

Above:
No. 915 *Brighton* and
No. 916 *Whitgift*
were built with a
chimney without a
capuchon. This
cannot have made
any noticeable
difference to the
performance of the
locomotives as they
were retained on
both but only fitted
to a few of the rest
of the class. (AC)

smokebox door. The iron on the left (looking at the front of the locomotive) replaced a small grabrail, used to pull open the smokebox door. In most cases, the lamp irons appear to have been repositioned at the same time that smoke deflectors were fitted but some locomotives had the lamp irons repositioned before receiving smoke deflectors.

On No. E900, no handrail was initially provided to assist staff climbing onto the front of the running plate by the front footsteps. On Nos. E901 to E909 and Nos. 910 to 939, small vertical stanchions were provided, adjacent to the lamp irons above each buffer. No. E900 later also received these stanchions, before smoke deflectors were fitted. These stanchions were removed from most of the class at around the time they were painted in the standard British Railways Dark Green livery, probably because the handholds in the front edge of the smoke deflector plates fulfilled the same function.

MAIN FRAMES

On Nos. E900 to E909, the area of the main frames between the cylinders and the buffer beam was covered by a number of snap-head rivets which were not apparent on Nos. 910 to 939. Presumably countersunk rivets were used on the later locomotives; it was just too early for such fabrications to be welded. In later

years, the maintenance records show that the frames required frequent attention due to fractures (cracking).

SANDING

Locomotives Nos. E900 to E909 were provided with gravity-fed sanding equipment, only in front of the leading driving wheels. This was found to be inadequate and sandboxes were added between the coupled wheels and steam-assisted sanding was provided in front of all four driving wheels. All photographs of Nos. E900 to E909 with smoke deflectors show sanding to all driving wheels, some locomotives received the modified sanding equipment before getting smoke deflectors. Although photographic evidence is lacking, it is thought that the second sandbox was added to some locomotives before steam sanding. Nos. 910 to 939 were built with steam sanding in front of all four driving wheels.

CABS

On Nos. E900 to E909, the lower edge of the cabside window was in line with the inward turn of the cabside with the top of the cabside cut-out in line with the top of the window. On Nos. 910 to 939, the cabside window and the top of the cut-out were raised by approximately 4in (10.2cm). The cabs of

Nos. 900 to 909 were never modified to the later arrangement. Nos. 910 to 939 were built with visors above the cabfront spectacles. Nos. 900 to 909 received these at about the same time as smoke-deflector plates were fitted, although a few photographs show locomotives with smoke deflectors but no visors.

During World War 2, the cabs were fitted with a blackout curtain, to make the firebox glow less visible from the air. When not in use, the curtain was rolled up on the rear edge of the cab, and could be unrolled and fixed to a framework on the front of the tender. The cabside window glasses were replaced by steel sheet. In November 1942, No. 931 *King's Wimbledon* was fitted with a cover over the cabside cut-out and a tender cab, to protect the enginemen if attacked by enemy aircraft. The covers were manufactured from plastic armour by the Neuchatel Asphalte Company. No other locomotives were fitted and the covers were removed in July 1944.

Bogie Springs and Frames

When new, the 'Schools' class locomotives were inclined to pitch on poor track. This was rectified by fitting stiffer coil springs to the bogie. There were also problems with bogie frames fracturing. The side frames of the bogies fitted initially to Nos. E900 to E909 and Nos. 910 to 921 had a shallow 'vee' form to the lower edge. From No. 923, the lower edge of the bogie frame was straight. No photographic evidence has been seen of which bogie frame was initially provided on No. 922. Earlier locomotives were all provided with straight-bottom bogie frames during the 1930s. The pattern of rivets was the same for both types of frame. It would appear that new frames were fitted to existing bogie centres.

Vacuum Pumps

The 'Schools' class locomotives were built with vacuum pumps, driven from the crosshead of the inside cylinder, to maintain brake vacuum whilst running. The pumps were removed in the early 1940s. The pumps were not visible from the side of the locomotive.

Piston Valve Lead

When 'Schools' class locomotives first entered service, problems were found in starting heavy trains, in particular when restarting 'up' trains around the curve out of London Bridge station. It was found that the lead on the valves was allowing too much steam to enter the cylinder, against the piston at the end of its stroke. The lead was reduced by altering the ends of the piston valves and the ring arrangement, an alteration not visible externally.

CHAPTER THREE

BULLEID MODIFICATIONS

The SR's new CME Oliver Bulleid made further
modifications to the 'Schools' class of locomotives and
further changes were made in British Railways service

When Oliver Bulleid succeeded Maunsell as Chief Mechanical Engineer of the Southern Railway in 1937, he began an immediate investigation into express locomotives designed by his predecessor. He was favourably impressed by the 'Schools' class, less impressed by the 'King Arthur' class, which he considered outdated, and definitely unimpressed by the four-cylinder 'Lord Nelson' 4-6-0s. To enable the 'Lord Nelsons' to reach full potential, he tried out a number of modifications, some of which were also applied to the 'Schools' class. Further modifications to 'Schools' were being applied during British Railways service.

STREAMLINING

Bulleid had been Sir Nigel Gresley's assistant on the London & North Eastern Railway (LNER) and had been closely involved with the introduction of the streamlined 'A4' Pacifics and other high-speed trains in LNER service. In February 1938, No. 935 *Sevenoaks* was fitted with a plywood and canvas casing at Eastleigh works and renumbered No. 999 Southern. The streamlining was similar to that on a 2-8-2 express locomotive which Bulleid had proposed in 1938, but which was not accepted by the civil engineer. There were at

least two versions of the streamlining, one including smoke deflectors plates. It is reported that the streamlined No. 999 Southern had one main line test run from Eastleigh to Micheldever, Hampshire, and back, a 32-mile (51.5km) round trip. It was converted back to standard as No. 935 *Sevenoaks* in April 1938.

CHIMNEYS

One of the more successful modifications to the 'Lord Nelson' class was to replace the single blastpipe and chimney with a Lemaître multiple-jet blastpipe and a large diameter chimney. Bulleid initiated a programme of fitting Lemaître exhausts to 'Schools' class locomotives. The first to be fitted was No. 914 *Eastbourne*, in January 1939. A tapered large-diameter chimney with no rim was fitted. The second of the class to be fitted with a Lemaître exhaust was No. 937 *Epsom* in May 1939 which had a straight chimney with no rim. No. 937 was also fitted with a new-type of Bulleid-designed cylinders. These had improved exhaust ports, which required the chimney to be moved forward on an extended smokebox. This was another modification which was applied to most of the 'Lord Nelsons' class, but was applied only to the one of the 'Schools' class.

Above:
When Bulleid took over the post of CME of the Southern Railway in 1937, he carried out some tests on the 'Schools'-class locomotives. No. 901 *Winchester* is at Cannon Street on the 18.15 to Ramsgate, July 1938 . The shelter on the front platform enabled test staff to take indicator diagrams showing the variation of the pressure in the cylinders during their stroke. (AC)

Left:
No. 931 *King's Wimbledon* was fitted with a Lemaître exhaust in July 1939 and was the first to carry the standard lipped chimney for Lemaître-fitted locomotives. It was also the only 'Schools' to run in full Maunsell livery with this type of exhaust. (RAS/JPW)

Below:
In February 1939, No. 914 *Eastbourne* was the first 'Schools' locomotive to be fitted with a Lemaître exhaust. (SLS)

The third 'Schools' with a Lemaître exhaust was No. 931 *King's Wimbledon* in July 1939. The locomotive retained the original cylinders and had a large-diameter lipped chimney. This was the only 'Schools' class locomotive to carry a Lemaître exhaust whilst still painted in full Maunsell-style livery. A further 17 of the class were fitted with Lemaître exhausts and lipped chimneys between 1940 and 1941. It was then decided not to rebuild any more of the class during wartime. No. 914 *Eastbourne* was fitted with a lipped chimney in July 1943 and

No. 937 *Epsom* in March 1944. No. 937 was refitted with Maunsell-type cylinders in 1841 and to a standard smokebox in December 1945.

Although it was generally considered that the 'Schools' locomotives with Lemaître exhausts were more powerful and free running than those unmodified, coal consumption was higher and it was found that unmodified locomotives were quite adequate for the traffic requirements. Twenty of the class therefore retained the single blastpipe and small chimney.

Don Bradley notes that in January 1946, No. 916 *Whitgift* and No. 926 *Repton* were fitted with Bulleid-type single blastpipes, designed to enable the locomotives to run on poor quality coal. A photograph of No. 916 shows that the chimney was not changed. Both were converted back to standard in May 1947 and November 1946.

BALANCING

In 1937, Harold Holcroft suggested to Bulleid that the balancing of the 'Schools' class should be altered, to eliminate all balance of reciprocating forces. In view of the largely self-balancing properties of a three-cylinder mechanism, it is surprising that balancing of the reciprocating forces had been incorporated in the initial design, but it was standard practice at the time. The fact that Holcroft suggested changing the balance immediately after Bulleid's arrival suggests that he may have been overruled at the design stage by Maunsell or by his assistant, James Clayton. One locomotive was modified, with no detriment to the ride. The change is visible in the shape of the balance weights on the driving wheels.

On the class as built, with the driving wheel crankpin at the bottom of the throw (at six o' clock) the balance weight is a crescent, incorporated into the wheel casting, covering six spoke gaps between twelve and three o'clock. On locomotives with modified balance, the outer cover of the weights is square-ended over four spoke gaps, with prominent rivet heads visible. The balance weights of the trailing coupled wheels were originally crescents incorporated into the wheel casting covering the four spoke gaps opposite the crankpin and were replaced by deeper, straight-edged, built-up balance weights in the same position. On No. 931, square-edged weights covering only two spoke gaps were fitted. In his memoirs, Holcroft states that only one locomotive was modified, but a study of photographs show that No. 931 *King's Wimbledon*, No. 932 *Blundells* and No. 937 *Epsom*

No. 929 *Malvern* passing Eastleigh with GWR carriage stock in 1938. (CR/PC)

all received modified balancing by 1939 although No. 931 and No. 932 later reverted to the original balancing arrangement. The modified balancing appears to have been applied over a number of years to approximately 10 locomotives but is not mentioned on the Engine Record Cards. In the tables, the date shown is that of the earliest photograph where rebalancing is visible.

SNIFTING VALVES

The Maunsell-type superheater, which was fitted to all 'Schools' class locomotives, had two snifting (anti-vacuum) valves, mounted on each side of the smokebox to the rear of the chimney. The valves were removed in the late 1940s.

SPEED RECORDERS

Bulleid had experience of the use of speed recorders on locomotives when working for LNER and decided to try the equipment out

on the SR. Twenty 'Schools' class and a number of other express locomotives were fitted with French-manufactured Flaman speed recorders in 1938-39. The speed recorder was located under the fireman's seat and recorded the speed of the locomotive on a paper roll. The drive to the equipment was taken from a crank on the crankpin of the rear right-hand driving wheel to a gearbox mounted on a bracket under the running plate. From this gearbox, a horizontal shaft drove the speed recorder. The Flaman speed recorders remained in use until 1940/41.

No. 939 *Leatherhead* was fitted with a Stone Deuta-type speedometer in 1938. This was driven from the crankpin of the left-hand rear driving wheel by a flexible cable to a gearbox. It indicated the speed on a dial in the cab. It was not satisfactory, and was disconnected after a short trial. In the late 1950s, British Railways began to install speedometers on express locomotives and 21 of the 'Schools' class were equipped between 1959 and 1960. These were supplied by J. Stones of Deptford which were

a development of the earlier type fitted to No. 939 *Leatherhead*.

AUTOMATIC WARNING SYSTEM

In the late 1950s, British Railways Automatic Warning System (AWS) was being installed on its main lines, including parts of the Southern Region. A receiver on the locomotive picked up signals from electro-magnets in the track at each signal. In the cab; at a clear signal, a bell rang. If the signal was at caution, the vacuum brake was applied, sounding a horn. (A total of 20 'Schools' class locomotives were fitted with AWS between 1959 and 1962.) The receiver was mounted on the bogie, with a protective plate below the buffer beam to prevent damage from the coupling. A battery box was mounted on the left-hand running plate, behind it was a cylindrical air reservoir. Although speedometers were fitted at around the same time as AWS, there were cases where locomotives were fitted with a speedometer but not AWS and vice versa.

INJECTORS

The 'Schools' class locomotives were built with a Gresham & Cravens No 11 live-steam injector mounted under the left-side of the cab and a Davies & Metcalfe No 10 Type H exhaust steam injector mounted under the right-side of the cab. In the late 1950s, Nos. 30906, 30907, 30913 and 30930 were provided with Davies & Metcalfe Type K exhaust steam injectors.

WATER TREATMENT

In April 1959, a start was made in providing 'Schools' class locomotives with the standard British Railways water treatment system, in which blocks of chemicals were placed in a feeder container on top of the tender. Apart from the container on top of the tender, the only visual sign was the addition of a yellow circle on the cabside, below the locomotive number. On the Western Region, this indicated a locomotive with less than 16-ton axle load, so the circle was replaced by a yellow triangle in 1961.

Above:
No. 30925 *Cheltenham* at Nine Elms, 30 May 1962. It is fitted with a BR speedometer, supplied by J. Stones. The generator is driven through a flexible cable from a gearbox which is driven by an arm on the left-hand trailing crankpin. Although no photograph is known, it is likely that the drive to the Stone Deuta speed recorder fitted to No. 939 *Leatherhead* in 1938 looked similar. The battery box, air reservoir and the conduit along the running plate valance show that it is fitted with AWS. (IA/JS)

CHAPTER FOUR

TENDERS

The 'Schools'-class locomotives were all
coupled to similar tenders but there were
some variations and tender exchanges.

At first sight, the 'Schools' class tender allocation was simplicity itself. With the exception of two late changes, all ran with similar 4,000-gallon (18,184 litre) six-wheel tenders built at Eastleigh Works. However, the early history of these tenders was far from simple and there were differences between the tenders coupled to each batch of locomotives.

TENDER TYPES

The tenders coupled to the 'Schools' class locomotives ran on six wheels and carried 4,000 gallons (18,184 litres) of water. Some tenders had spoked and some had disc wheels. Compared with the previous Ashford pattern 3,500-gallon (15,911-litre) tender, the new 4,000-gallon (18,184-litre) tender had a wider tank with the platform at the Eastleigh standard height of 4ft (1.22m) above the rail. Unlike the 3,500-gallon (15,911-litre) tenders, the frames were not slotted. The first of these tenders were ordered for a batch of ten of the 'King Arthur' class, which were then cancelled in favour of the larger 'Lord Nelson' class. These six-wheel tenders were initially coupled to two of the 'Lord Nelson' class and to some existing 'King Arthurs'.

In 1930, the six-wheeled tenders coupled to 'Lord Nelson' No. E852 and 'King Arthurs' Nos E768 and Nos. E770, 771 and 772 were replaced by new bogie-type tenders. The six wheelers were rebuilt with turned in coal plates and coupled to 'Schools' class Nos. E905 to E909. This resulted in the tenders attached to Nos. E905 to E909 having straight-edged footstep backing plates, to match those on the 'King Arthurs'. The tenders coupled to Nos. E900 to E904 and Nos. 910 to 939 had curved backing plates to the footsteps, matching those on the locomotives. These footsteps remained unchanged throughout the life of the tenders, but some late tender exchanges resulted in 'straight step' tenders being attached to other 'Schools' class locomotives. It would appear that the turned in coal plates on 'Schools'-class tenders were provided to match the shape of the cab as the 'N1'-class 2-6-0s, which were within the Hastings line loading gauge, had similar tenders with straight coal plates.

The tenders attached to Nos. E900 to E909 had a pair of toolboxes, set lengthwise, one on each side at the front of the tender. The tenders attached to Nos. 910 to 939 had larger toolboxes set transversely across the front of the tender. When tender numbers were allocated in the early 1930s, the tenders attached to the 'Schools' class locomotives were numbered Nos. 700 to 739 in locomotive order, including those yet to be built.

There were initially three variants of 4,000-gallon (18,184-litre) tender coupled to the

Above:
No. E900 *Eton* on display at Windsor & Eton Riverside on 28 or 29 March 1930. The bufferbeams of E900 and E901 carried LSWR-style sans serif numerals. The tender carries a brass numberplate on the rear, similar to those on the cabside. The wheels on the tender are spoked. (RAS/BW)

Left:
Tender 708 on E908 *Westminster* at New Cross, 24 October 1930. The pre-used tenders of E905 to E909 had straight-edged footstep backing plates. The longitudinal toolboxes are visible. (RAS/OJM)

Right:
No. 921 *Shrewsbury* at Bricklayers' Arms. Note the serif-style numerals on the rear of the tender body, the standard arrangement after elimination of the E prefix. The tender has disc wheels. (RAS/RSC)

Right:
No. 917 *Ardingly* passing Bromley on a down train in the mid-1930s. The number on the rear of the tender is below the upper footstep. (HCC)

Right:
No. 926 *Repton* at Nine Elms, 29 August 1935. The tender was built with SKF roller-bearing axleboxes. These were not satisfactory and were replaced by standard axleboxes in March 1936. (AC)

Left:
No. 30908 *Westminster* passing Tonbridge on the 14.10 Hastings to Charing Cross, 6 August 1949. No. 30908 is in BR black with an unlettered tender. The tender was fitted with Isothermos-type roller-bearing axleboxes from June 1932 to April 1951. (DLB)

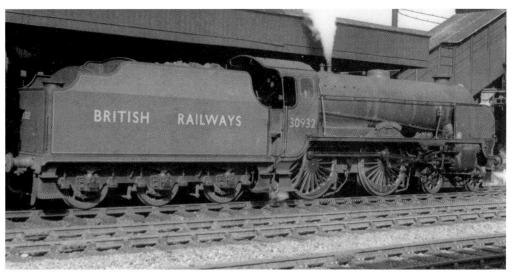

Left:
Self-trimming tender 732 is coupled to No. 30932 *Blundells*. The original rear coal bulkhead is retained but another is provided at the rear of the raised bunker. No. 30932 is in Malachite Green with 'BRITISH RAILWAYS' in Gill Sans-style lettering but the number on the rear of the tender is in Bulleid-style numerals. (DLB)

'Schools' class locomotives:

Locomotives   Tenders
Nos. E900 to E904   Nos. 700 to 704
Curved footstep backing plates and lengthwise-mounted toolboxes
Nos. E905 to E909   Nos. 705 to 709
Straight footstep backing plates and lengthwise-mounted toolboxes
Nos. 910 to 939   Nos. 710 to 739
Curved footstep backing plates and transverse-mounted toolboxes

ROLLER BEARINGS

Three 'Schools' class tenders ran for a time with roller-bearing axleboxes.

Tender No. 708, coupled to No. 908 *Westminster*, was fitted with Isothermos-type axleboxes in June 1932. These were successful and ran until replaced by standard axleboxes in April 1951. Tenders Nos. 714 and 726, coupled to No. 914 *Eastbourne* and No. 926 *Repton*, were built new with SKF roller-bearing type axleboxes. These were not successful and were replaced by standard axleboxes in June and March 1936 respectively.

SELF-TRIMMING BUNKER

One of Bulleid's modifications to the 'Lord Nelsons' class was to raise the angle of the bottom of the coal bunker to make it 'self trimming'. This modification had been initiated in Maunsell's days. As the coal at the front of the tender was shovelled out, that behind fell into its place, so the fireman did not need to bring coal forward from the back of the tender and could spend all his energy in

firing the long awkward grate of a 'Lord Nelson' locomotive. The coal plates at the side of the tender were raised to enclose the higher bunker.

In July 1938, Bulleid carried out a similar modification to tender No. 732 attached to No. 932 *Blundells*. The modification was not necessary on the shorter tender of the 'Schools', besides which the easily fired grate of the 'Schools' class gave the fireman a much easier life than that of the 'Lord Nelson'.

No further 'Schools' were modified but tender No. 732 remained as a self-trimming type. In August 1958, locomotive No. 30932 *Blundells* exchanged tenders with No. 30905 *Tonbridge* which then ran with the self-trimming tender. This tender change was carried out because Ashford had repainted the tender green, whilst No. 30932 remained in black livery.

There were a number of tender exchanges between 'Schools' class locomotives, particularly

during the 1950s. In most cases, the tenders exchanged were of the same type but No. 30903 *Charterhouse* and No. 30906 *Sherborne* exchanged straight and curved footstep tenders in April 1962.

LORD NELSON TENDERS

Right at the end of their existence, two 'Schools' class locomotives received high-sided bogie tenders from withdrawn 'Lord Nelson' locomotives. No. 30912 *Downside* received tender No. 1012 from No. 30865 *Sir John Hawkins* in July 1961 and No. 30921 *Shrewsbury* received tender No. 1007 from No. 30854 *Howard of Effingham* in November 1961. It is understood that this change was made to improve braking when working freight trains, it would also have increased the range of the 'Schools' class on the longer runs of the Western section but prevented use of the 50ft (15.24m) turntables.

Right:
Detail of axlebox
and spring on tender
718 whilst at
Eastleigh, 29 October
1949. A SE&CR-type
axlebox cover (a
detail only for the
most purist of
modellers) has been
fitted. (AEW/SWC)

Right:
No. 30913 *Christ's
Hospital* being filled
with water at
Bricklayers' Arms,
15 May 1949. The
tender is lettered in
Gill Sans characters
but with Bulleid-style
numerals on the rear.
(AEW/SWC)

Left:
No. 30921 *Shrewsbury* passing Winchester on the 12.00 Waterloo to Lymington Pier, 18 August 1962. In November 1961, it was coupled to bogie tender 1007 from 'Lord Nelson' class No. 30854 *Howard of Effingham*. This prevented it from being turned on the Brockenhurst turntable. It has been reported that No. 30921 ran tender first from Brockenhurst to turn on the triangle at Northam. No. 30921 then took over its train, the 15.30 from Lymington Pier, from a relief locomotive at Southampton. (AC)

S15 CLASS

The tenders from two 'Schools' class locomotives were later attached to Maunsell 'S15' class small wheeled 4-6-0s. In May 1962, tender No. 708 from the withdrawn No. 30908 *Westminster* was attached to 'S15' No. 30833 and ran until May 1965. In June 1962, tender No. 712 displaced when No. 30912 *Downside* received a 'Lord Nelson'-type tender, was attached to 'S15' No. 30837 and ran until September 1965.

No. 30926 REPTON

Whilst the preserved No. 30926 *Repton* was running in Canada, its tender was rebuilt with higher sides and rear coal bulkhead to give greater weather protection to the crew when running tender first. When the locomotive arrived on the North Yorkshire Moors Railway, the higher sides and rear coal bulkhead were retained, but the sides were modified to fall in two steps at the rear, similar but not identical to tender No. 732.

Left:
Tender 712 of No. 30912 *Downside* at Stewart's Lane, 25 August 1950. The tender is in BR lined black with the small early totem and has spoked wheels. (AEW/SWC)

CHAPTER FIVE

LIVERIES

The 'Schools' class of locomotives were initially painted green
then black then green then black and then back to green again.
Not all entered the second or third green periods.

In service, the 'Schools' class ran in a number of liveries. From 1930 to 1942 they were green, but with considerable variety after 1938. Between 1942 and 1946 all were repainted black until green returned from 1946 to 1948. From late 1948 to 1956, the livery was once more black, then reverting to green for the last few years. Not all locomotives received green in the two post-war green periods.

Maunsell Liveries

All the 'Schools' class locomotives were initially painted in Maunsell's Dark Green livery. Cab, splasher, footplate valance and tender sides were dark green, with a fine white line between the green and the black edging. Boiler bands were black with a fine white line either side, but with only one white line at the rear of the smokebox. Similar banding was applied to the front and rear vertical edges of the green painted cylinders, but was replaced by a rectangular panel in the late 1930s. Wheels were painted green, with black tyres and axle ends.

The Southern Railway did not initially renumber its inherited locomotives, but added a prefix to the number, A (Ashford) for ex-SE&CR locomotives, B (Brighton) for ex-LB&SCR locomotives and E (Eastleigh) for ex-LSWR locomotives. New locomotives were numbered into the appropriate series depending on which works they were allocated to for overhaul. The first ten 'Schools' had E prefix numbers Nos. E900 to E909. In 1931, the Southern abandoned prefixes, E series locomotives retaining their existing numbers whilst 1000 was added to most A series numbers, 2000 to B series numbers and 3000 to LSWR duplicate numbers. Nos. E900 to E909 lost the prefixes and Nos. 910 to 939 never had the prefix.

The number was carried on the cabside by an oval brass numberplate, $13^5/8$ x $7^5/8$in (34.61 x 19.37cm) with the lettering 'SOUTHERN RAILWAY' in an arc around the top of the plate with the number below and the prefix between. A third plate was attached to the rear of the tender body. When the prefixes were abandoned, the E-prefix on the cabside plates was ground off and the plate on the rear of the tender was replaced by painted numerals. Nos. 900 to 939 received cabside plates with 'SOUTHERN' in an arc at the top of the plate, 'RAILWAY' at the bottom and the number between. The backing colour of the name and numberplates was red, using the same vermilion colour, with a tint of orange, as was used for the buffer beams, and remained so into early British Railways days.

Nos. E900 and E901 initially had L&SWR-style sans serif buffer beam numerals in gilt with E to the left of the coupling hook and the number

Above:
No. 933 *King's Canterbury* at Bournemouth Central on an up express in 1936, with two Maunsell open thirds at the front of the train. The additional train number board suggests that it is a summer Saturday. A Drummond 'T14' 4-6-0 waits in the bay to take over a later train. Both locomotives and carriages are in Maunsell Green livery. (CR/JK)

Left:
No. 926 *Repton* arriving at Bournemouth Central on a down express in 1936 as a Bournemouth Corporation trolley-bus passes over on the Holdenhurst Road bridge. (CR/JK)

Right:
No. 912 *Downside*, repainted in Olive green livery with dark green edging and yellow lining, April 1939. From early 1939, Bulleid's liveries included black cylinders and lined green smoke deflector plates. (SLS)

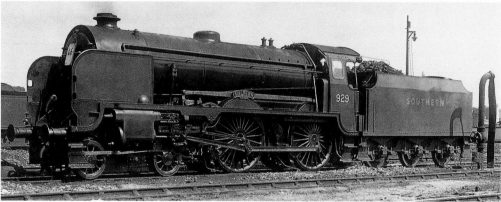

Right:
No. 929 *Malvern*, at Nine Elms, probably during the summer of 1939. First painted Malachite Green style in 1938 and later repainted Malachite Green with black edging and yellow lining, June 1939. The cylinders are now black and the smoke deflector plates are green. This became the standard 'Schools' livery until 1942. The photograph was taken before March 1941 when No. 929 was fitted with a Lemaître exhaust. (SLS)

to the right. Nos. E902 to E909 had yellow serif lettering in the same layout. Locomotives Nos. 910 to 939, and 900 to 909 when repainted, had serif lettering in yellow but with 'N°' to the left of the coupling hook, in place of the suffix. The Western Section power classification A was painted in white on the running plate valance, above the front footsteps.

Tender lettering comprised the word 'SOUTHERN', 9ft 9in (2.97m) long in elongated 6½in (16.5cm) serif letters. The locomotive number was applied below it in 1ft 6in (45.7cm) block figures, with the 3in (7.6cm) E prefix in between. The lettering and numbers were painted in a primrose colour. Nos. E900 to E909 carried a third numberplate, similar to those on the cabside, on the rear of the tender. When the E-prefixes were abandoned, the numbers on the sides of the tender were moved up slightly. The numberplates on the rear of the tenders were replaced by transfer-applied numerals.

▌BULLEID LIVERIES

In May 1938, the Southern's new CME, Oliver Bulleid, initiated an assortment of brighter liveries

for the Southern Railway's locomotives. After initial trials with 'King Arthur'-class locomotive No. 749 *Iseult*, which did not go to traffic in the new livery, a bright green livery was applied to seven of 'Schools' class (Nos. 925 to 930 and 932) in July and August 1938 at Bournemouth, regardless of whether the locomotives were due for a repaint. The green was initially known as 'Bournemouth Green', but later became known as Malachite Green. The style and position of the lining was still as on Maunsell livery, with black edging and white lining, but the lettering style and arrangement was changed. The running number was painted on to the cabside in place of the numberplate and the word 'SOUTHERN' was placed centrally on the vertical part of the tender side. The sans serif block letters were painted in gilt, with a fine body colour line inside the letters. Numerals were shaded black and did not have the body coloured inside line. Six sets of carriages, forming two 11-coach trains, were also repainted in the same green for the Waterloo-Bournemouth services.

After this initial livery trial, seven 'Schools' class locomotives were repainted in Maunsell Green but with the new lettering style, and two more in the Malachite Green. On all these locomotives,

Left:
No. 927 *Clifton* in Malachite Green livery, ready to leave Waterloo in August 1938. The front of the locomotive is in sunlight and the shade of the Malachite Green does not appear greatly different from that used during the post-war period. (CR/HML)

Centre:
No. 927 *Clifton* in Malachite Green in 1938. Comparison with the photograph below shows the difficulty in trying to ascertain the colour of a locomotive from a black and white photograph. Both photographs show the same locomotive in the same livery, but the apparent shade is totally different. In this case, orthochromatic film was used and the sun was not directly on the side of the locomotive. (SLS)

Left:
No. 927 *Clifton* at Eastleigh on a Bournemouth train in 1938. It is finished in Malachite Green whilst the carriages are still in Maunsell Dark Green. With the sun on the side of the train, the panchromatic film used by the photographer shows the locomotive as being painted in a very light shade. (SLS)

until early 1939, smoke deflectors were painted black and cylinder casings were green with a lining panel, then black. In May 1939, a further series of experimental liveries were applied in which the cylinder casings were black and the smoke deflectors, above the level of the running plate above the cylinders, were lined green. These liveries included three variants of an olive green, sometimes called 'Dover Green' and further applications of the Malachite Green.

Liveries with Green cylinders and Black smoke deflectors

(a) Malachite Green with black edging and white lining in July and August 1938 on locomotives Nos. 925 to 930 and No. 932, also Nos. 906, 921 and 938 in April 1939.

(b) Maunsell Green with black edging and white lining from November 1938 to March 1939 on locomotives Nos. 908, 914, 923, 924, 933 and 934. Locomotive Nos. 914, 923 and 933 were finished with black painted cylinders.

Liveries with Black cylinders and Green smoke deflectors

(c) Olive Green with dark green edging and yellow lining, used in May 1939 on No. 912.

(d) Malachite Green with black edging and white lining, in June 1939 on No. 937.

Right:
No. 905 *Tonbridge* at Eastleigh. It was repainted in Malachite Green in December 1946 and retained this, still with a Southern number, until repainted lined black in September 1949. (CR/ST)

Right:
No. 30919 *Harrow* at Eastleigh after an overhaul at the works in January 1957, newly repainted in lined black with the small first BR totem. No power classification is displayed. (CR)

(e) Olive Green with black edging and yellow lining, from March to June 1940 on Nos. 900, 902, 911, 917, 918, 920, and 927.

(f) Malachite Green with green edging and yellow lining in June 1939 on Nos. 919, 925 and 935.

(g) Malachite Green with black edging and yellow lining, from July 1939 to April 1942 on all 'Schools' class locomotives except for Nos. 900, 902, 906, 917, 918 and 920. This became the standard livery until unlined black was adopted.

The photographers of the day flocked to record the Bournemouth-based 'Schools' locomotives in the new livery, but there is considerable variation in what is shown by their black and white photographs. Some appear to be startlingly light

whilst others appear to be dark. This is probably due the orthochromatic and panchromatic films of the time reacting differently to the colours. It is generally accepted that the early Malachite Green was lighter than that used later but exactly when it changed is not clear.

In 1941, the lettering was changed to the 'Sunshine' style. Both the numerals and the word 'SOUTHERN' were now shaded, gilt finished characters with black shading on green locomotives and golden yellow painted characters with green shading on black locomotives. The scarcity of photographs from this period precludes any totally authoritative statement on liveries, but it is not thought that 'Sunshine'-style lettering was used on repaints to livery (g) during 1941/42.

Between June 1942 and March 1946, all repaints were in unlined black with green shaded 'Sunshine'-style lettering.

From January 1946, Malachite Green began to be used again, to livery variant (g), with black shaded yellow painted 'Sunshine'-style lettering. Wheels were still generally painted green, but footstep backing plates and the fronts of the cabs were now black. On all the pre-war green liveries, the lining of the running plate valance followed the whole shape of the bracket carrying the expansion link pivot. On post-war repaints, the line went straight across the lower edge of the bracket, above the expansion link pivot. Some of the class did not receive Malachite Green until early British Railways days and eight locomotives

were not painted in post-war Malachite Green livery at all.

There were two non-standard applications of the post-war Malachite Green. No. 934 *St Lawrence* was the first green repaint in January 1946 and had lined green footstep backing plates and the pre-war style valance lining. No. 919 *Harrow* was repainted at Ashford with black smoke deflectors, a green cab front and lined green painted cylinders and footstep backing plates.

▎BRITISH RAILWAYS LIVERIES

For the first ten months of British Railways ownership, the livery applied to the 'Schools' was the Southern Malachite Green, but with various

Right:
No. 901 *Winchester* near Hildenborough on a Hastings to Charing Cross train in 1946. It is in unlined black livery which was retained until receiving BR lined black in October 1948. The plated-over cab windows and blackout curtain are still in positon. The first and third carriages are 9 ft wide, so must have been added to the train at Tonbridge. (IA/ET)

Right:
No. 930 *Radley* at Nine Elms in the unlined black livery applied to 'Schools' class locomotives between 1942 and 1946. Lettering is green shaded 'Sunshine' style. The cabside window opening has been plated in steel and a blackout curtain is rolled up on the front of the tender. (IA)

lettering schemes. Generally, full repaints only occurred at full overhauls but partial repaints, such as adding 30xxx numbers, also occurred during light repairs at Eastleigh, Ashford and Brighton sheds. Dates of renumbering were recorded on the Engine Record Cards. Three 'Schools' loco-motives ran with s-prefix numbers, s914 *Eastbourne*, s934 *St. Lawrence* and s938 *St. Olave's*. Until October 1948, repaints were in Malachite Green, but with a variety of lettering arrange-ments. Liveries noted at the time of locomotives receiving British Railways numbers were:

(h) Malachite Green with the 30xxx number added to the Southern livery, July 1948-March 1949 on Nos. 30902, 30909, 30912, 30920, 30924 and 30936.

(i) Malachite Green with BRITISH RAILWAYS in 'Sunshine'-style lettering, March-September 1948 on s914, s934 (later No. 30934), s938, Nos. 30900, 30903, 30904, 30917, 30919, 30926, 30933 and 30939.

(j) Malachite Green with BRITISH RAILWAYS in Gill sans lettering, July to October 1948 on Nos. 30907, 30913, 30928, 30930, 30932 and 30937

A number of the class painted in both green and black liveries were not renumbered until after the British Railways lined black livery was introduced. No. 30908 *Westminster* was the only 'Schools'- class locomotive to receive a British Railways number on the unlined black Southern livery.

The 'BRITISH RAILWAYS' in 'Sunshine' style was produced by using letters where these were available from the existing 'SOUTHERN'

Left:
No. 902 *Wellington* at Waterloo East on the 08.25 Charing Cross to Hastings, 1948. No. 902 was painted post-war Malachite Green livery in June 1946. The footstep backing plates and the front of the cab are now black. (IA/GJR)

Above:
No. 919 *Harrow* at Victoria, 14 July 1947. It was repainted in Malachite Green at Ashford in May 1946 with black smoke deflector plates, green panelled cylinders, green footstep backing plates and cab front. (RAS/JPW)

transfers, with the others letters being hand painted. The cabside numerals were in Bulleid-style numerals when 'Sunshine' lettering was applied on the tender, and in Gill sans numerals when the tender was lettered in Gill sans. Bulleid numerals were still used on the rear of tenders when the lettering on the side was in Gill sans. Bulleid cabside numerals were usually 9in (22.8cm) high but Nos. 30900, 30903, 30904, 30919, 30926 and 30939 had 6in (15.2cm) cabside numerals and No. 30903, which was renumbered at Brighton, had the cabside number shown as No. 30,903. Gill sans-style cabside numerals were 10in (24.5cm) high on Malachite Green finished 'Schools' locomotives. Smokebox number plates were fitted from September 1948, but were also added to locomotives in the earlier liveries during intermediate works visits.

From October 1948 until July 1956, all repaints were in British Railways standard black with red, cream and grey lining, basically the livery of the London & North Western Railway. The following lettering variants appeared:

(k) Lined black with 'BRITISH RAILWAYS' in Gill sans lettering, October-November 1948 on Nos. 30901, 30916, 30923 and 30931.

(l) Lined black with no tender lettering, November 1948-August 1949 on Nos. 30905, 30908, 30910, 30911, 30915, 30922, 30926, 30928, 30929, 30935, 30936 and 30938.

(m) Lined black with first British Railways totem from September 1949 to June 1956.

On the 'BRITISH RAILWAYS' lettered locomotives, the cabside lining went over the top

Right:
No. 30932 *Blundells* at Eastleigh in 1954, painted in lined black with 8in (20.3cm) cabside numerals and the small first BR totem. Note with the high-sided tender, the totem has been raised to a position level with the cabside numerals. (CR)

Right:
No. 30926 *Repton* in clean condition at Stewarts Lane, 28 June 1960, probably ready for Derby day. The conduit on the buffer beam shows that it is fitted with AWS. Also overhead electrification warning signs are fitted. The nameplate has a red background . (CR)

Right:
No. 30926 *Repton* at Ashford, 25 February 1962. The balance weights on the wheels are clearly visible, square ended on the driving axle and crescent-shaped on the coupled axle. No. 30926 is fitted with both AWS and speedometer. (CR)

Left:
No. 30925 *Cheltenham* at London Bridge. It is probably on empty stock as the headcode is for New Cross via Bricklayers' Arms. The photograph is undated but could be not long after No. 30925 received green livery, AWS and a speedometer in January 1960. The nameplates have a red background. Also the motion brackets are painted red. (CR)

Left:
No. 30936 *Cranleigh* at Ashford, September 1960. A left-facing second small totem is on the tender. Note the electrification warning sign on the rear of the tender, in addition to those on the smoke deflector plates and firebox cladding. (CR)

Left:
Early in 1948, three 'Schools' locomotives were used to try out possible lettering styles for the newly formed British Railways. The tender of No. 926 *Repton* received the early British Railways lettering, as used on notepaper and publicity material. (IA)

of the cabside window but on later repaints, this was limited to a panel on the lower part of the cabside.

Initially, the tender lining on all three livery variants following the shape of the coal plates, and the large first British Railways totem was used in livery (m). From March 1950, the upper edge of the tender lining was below the turn in of the coal plates and the small totem was used. Some locomotives with unlettered tenders later received the small totem whilst retaining full-depth tender lining. The first 31 black repaints had 10in (25.4cm) cabside numerals but these were later reduced to 8in (20.3cm).

There were detail differences in the way the lining was applied, both on the tender and on the running plate valance. On some locomotives, with

either the large or small BR totem, the line carried straight across the expansion link bracket. None of the black repaints incorporated the second-style British Railways totem. With the black livery, the Western Section A power classification was moved from the front of the running plate valance to the cabside, below the number. It was omitted on Ashford repaints. British Railways standard oval shed plates were attached to smokebox doors from around August 1950. The plates were fitted at running sheds as well as at works, and soon appeared on all locomotives.

In June 1956, overhauls to 'Schools'-class locomotives were transferred from Eastleigh to Ashford. At the same time, the livery was changed to the BR Dark Green with orange and black lining, basically the livery of the Great Western

Left:
When No. 903 *Charterhouse* received the British Railways number 30,903 at Brighton, March 1948, in 6in (15.24cm) numerals. Brighton used a similar style on a number of ex-LB&SCR locomotives. The odd number was still there when 30,903 next visited Eastleigh works on 19 February 1949. (SLS/AJC)

Left:
No. 30939 *Leatherhead* was repainted at Eastleigh in April 1948, with 'BRITISH RAILWAYS' in Bulleid-style characters on the tender and 6in (15.24cm) cabside numerals . Nos 30900, 30903, 30904, 30919, and 30926 received similar numerals at Brighton. (AEW/SWC)

Railway. Cabside numerals, sized 8in (20.3cm), were used on all dark green painted 'Schools'. Initial green repaints still carried the first small BR totem on the tender but the large second type of totem was applied from March 1957. This totem was applied with the heraldically incorrect right-facing lion on the righthand side of the tender until late 1958. Left facing lions subsequently were placed on both sides. On all dark green repaints, the lining on the running plate valance cut straight across the expansion link bracket, the lower part of which was painted black. The lining on the cabside did not follow the shape of the running plate but was a rectangle, with the running plate drop cutting into it. On some green painted 'Schools', the motion bracket was picked out in red. On green repaints, the A power

classification was replaced by 5P, above the number. Some photographs show 5P on black locomotives but this might be a subsequent re-lettering to the existing livery.

Nameplates had a red background until 1952, when BR headquarters ruled that all nameplates should have a black background. This ruling was generally followed for main works repaints until the early 1960s, but many of the running sheds repainted the nameplates red. From 1961, a few of the remaining 'Schools' received the standard white with a red lightning flash, overhead electrification warning plates. These were fitted to the lower front portion of the smoke deflectors, to the firebox cladding, adjacent to the cab front spectacles and on the rear of the tender, below the top lamp bracket .

Right:
No. 30902 *Wellington* at Nine Elms, September 1962. It is fitted with AWS but no speedometer. There are no electrification warning signs but the yellow spot denoting water treatment has been replaced by a triangle. (CR/WP)

Right:
No. 30901 *Winchester* at Stewarts Lane in June 1962, cleaned as standby locomotive for the Derby Day royal train to Tattenham Corner. It has AWS and speedometer but no electrification warning signs or red motion bracket. (CR/JFWP)

Right:
No. 30924 *Haileybury* at Ashford shed in June 1961. It has a red background to the nameplate and red motion bracket but neither a speedometer nor AWS, which were never fitted. (CR/AS)

Left:
No. 30934 *St Lawrence* at Basingstoke, 4 August 1962. It has both AWS and speedometer, also electrification warning signs on the firebox cladding. Note the clean(er) patch on the smoke deflector plate where the warning sign appears to have fallen off. (CR)

Left:
No. 30912 *Downside* and 2-6-0 'N' class No. 31414 at Ashford Works in June 1960. Both have been fitted with AWS equipment. The 'bash' plates in front of the AWS receivers have been primed but not yet painted black, so are more visible than in most photographs. (CR)

Left:
No. 30913 *Christ's Hospital* at Southampton Central in April 1960. It has arrived on a down van train and the fireman is removing the route indicator discs. It is fitted with AWS but no speedometer. (CR)

Right:
No. 30937 *Epsom*, recently repainted in Malachite Green livery with 'BRITISH RAILWAYS' and numerals in Gill Sans lettering. Eastleigh, 27 March 1949. (RKB)

Right:
No. 30931 *King's Wimbledon* at Eastleigh, 12 November 1949. The first four 'Schools' to be repainted into British Railways lined black livery in October and November 1948 had the tender lettering 'BRITISH RAILWAYS' in Gill Sans. On these four locomotives, the cabside lining went over the window. The splashers were not lined. (RKB/WG)

Right:
No. 30911 *Dover* at Eastleigh, 28 August 1949, repainted into British Railways lined black livery. The cabside lining is limited to a panel below the window. The 'A' power classification is now below the number. (RKB/WG)

Right:
No. 30919 *Harrow*, in December 1949 repainted in lined black livery with the large first totem. The tender lining follows the whole of the tender side and the lining on the running plate valance follows the widening by the motion bracket. (BR)

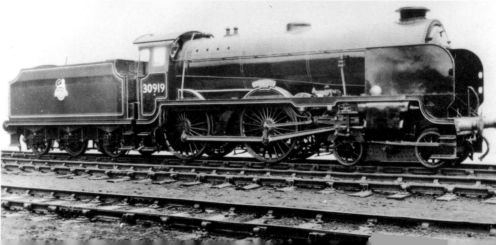

Left:
No. 30934
St Lawrence at
Ashford, 19 April
1954, part repainted
in lined black with
small first totem, 8in
(20.3cm) cabside
numerals and no
power classification.
The tender lining
differs from the
Eastleigh style.
(RKB/WG)

Left:
No. 30932 *Blundells*
at Eastleigh,
27 March 1954, in
BR lined black with
small first totem and
8in (20.3cm) cab
numerals. On the
high-sided tender,
the totem has been
raised to the level of
the cabside numerals.
(RKB/EWF)

Left:
No. 30907 *Dulwich*
at Weymouth,
23 June 1957. It was
repainted in BR Dark
Green livery with the
small early totem at
Ashford, July 1957.
The cabside numerals
are lowered with
the 5P power
classification above.
(AEW/SWC)

Right:
No. 30927 *Clifton* at
Ashford on a train to
Canterbury West and
Ramsgate. It received
Dark Green livery at
Ashford in March
1958. It has the second
British Railways crest
on the tender, with the
heraldically incorrect
right facing lion on
the right-hand side.
(IA/DCO)

CHAPTER SIX

ALLOCATION

The 'Schools' class ran on the main lines of all
three sections of the Southern Railway but
were predominantly Eastern section locomotives

Although generally associated with the Eastern section of the Southern Railway, the 'Schools' also ran on the Central and Western sections. With a 21-ton axle loading, the class were always main-line locomotives. Three main factors governed where the 'Schools' class were allocated: loading gauge restrictions, turntable lengths and electrification. The restricted loading gauge of the Tonbridge-Hastings, Kent lines gave the class a virtual monopoly of passenger working until diesel units arrived in 1958. The SR had a number of short (nominal 50ft [15.24m]) turntables at important locations, which could not be used by 4-6-0 locomotives. There were generally shunting triangles available in the vicinity which could be used, but with the inconvenience of having to use busy running lines for turning light engines. Availability of the 'Schools' class enabled modern express locomotives to be turned at these locations.

Electrification was the spectre hanging over the future of all SR steam locomotives throughout the existence of the company and into British Railways days. In 1930, the Southern Electric was purely a suburban operation and the only steam locomotives displaced had been the numbers of suburban tank engines owned by all three constituent companies of the Southern Railway. During the 1930s, all the main lines

of the Central section were electrified and electrification on the Eastern and Western sections was extending into areas where tender locomotives would previously have been used.

EASTERN SECTION

The Eastern section of the Southern Railway was the main area of activity of the 'Schools' class until almost the end of service. After a history of trying to bankrupt each other by running competitive services to almost every town in the county of Kent, the South Eastern Railway (SER) and the London Chatham & Dover Railway (LC&DR) had finally reached a working agreement, under a joint managing committee, in 1899. By the time the Southern Railway had taken over in 1923, some rationalisation and infrastructure improvement had occurred but many of the main lines in Kent were still subject to restrictive axle-weight limits due to lack of past investment. At the time of their introduction in 1930, the 'Schools' could run only over the old SER main line from London to Dover and Deal via Ashford. Nos. E900 to E903, also Nos. E905 and E906, were allocated new to Dover and based at the sub shed at Deal, which had a 50ft (15.24m) turntable, to work express passenger trains to Charing Cross, London.

Above:
No. 30930 *Radley* on Somerhill Bank, between Tonbridge and Tunbridge Wells, on the 17.25 (FO) Charing Cross to Hastings train in May 1957. The close track spacing is very apparent, the usual 6ft (1.83m) way between up and down tracks being more like 5ft (1.52m). (CR/NS)

Left:
No. 30924 *Haileybury* passing Bromley South on a London Bridge to Dover train in 1957. Even if it had been cleaned, No. 30924 would still be black. Trainset 235 is an eight-car set of Maunsell 9ft (2.74m) wide carriages with no catering provision. (CR)

Right:
E900 *Eton* near Chelsfield on a Victoria to Dover express via Chatham. E900 is as built but is now fitted with the stanchions above the buffers which were provided from new on all the other 'Schools' class locomotives. (RKB)

Right:
E902 *Wellington* on a Victoria to Dover express via Chatham, circa 1931. E902 is largely as built, but has gained rear wheel sanding. The train consists of Maunsell's Restriction 1 (8ft 6in [2.6m] wide) carriages built for the Kent main lines and a Pullman car. (AC)

During 1930, improvements to the old LC&DR main line from Victoria, London to Ramsgate via Chatham, Kent and the construction of a new connection at Minster, between Deal and Ramsgate, allowed the class to work from London to Ramsgate either via Dover or via Chatham. Deal shed was closed and its 'Schools' were transferred to Ramsgate. In mid-1931, improvements to the Tonbridge-Hastings line permitted the class to be run over the line. The running shed for Hastings was St. Leonards, with a 50ft (15.24m) turntable. By 1933, when the second batch of 'Schools' had been delivered, nine were based at Ramsgate and eleven at St. Leonard's. When all 40 of the class were in service,

Ramsgate and St Leonard's had 12 each and six were at Bricklayers' Arms (Bermondsey, south London), the first time any 'Schools' class locomotives had been based at any London shed.

The war years 1939 to 1945 saw considerable moving around of locomotives. Being close to the war zone, any unnecessary travel in Kent was severely discouraged and a number of the class on the Eastern Section were moved west. After the war all were returned and by 1949, were in service on the Eastern section. The introduction of diesel-electric multiple-units on the Hastings line in 1958 and electrification of the Kent Coast main lines via Chatham in 1959 and via Ashford in 1961 signalled the end of steam services.

CENTRAL SECTION

The Central section of the SR (the old London Brighton & South Coast Railway) was an early recipient of 'Schools' class locomotives, with Nos. E904, E907 to E909 being allocated when new to Eastbourne for express services to London Bridge and Victoria. By 1933, these had been replaced by Nos. 913 to 916 (including No. 914 *Eastbourne*). Electrification of the line from London to Eastbourne and Hastings in 1935 took over the 'Schools' work and none was then based on the Central section, although the many connections in the London area permitted frequent special workings over Central section lines. Nos. 928 to 930 were based at Brighton

briefly during 1946, working through trains to the Western section along the South Coast line. Although Stewarts Lane, Battersea, London was basically an Eastern section shed, it provided motive power for steam workings over the Central section after the electrification of the main lines. Newhaven boat trains and the annual Royal Train to Tattenham Corner, Epsom, Surrey for the Derby became regular 'Schools' prestige appearances, together with many less prestigious jobs such as parcels trains.

With the electrification of the main lines in Kent, the class was returned to the Central section. In 1960, Nos. 30900 to 30902 and Nos. 30917 to 30919 were at Brighton and Nos. 30914 to 30916 at Redhill. Duties included

Right:
No. 914 *Eastbourne* passing Chelsfield on a Charing Cross to Hastings train, some time after 1935. This was when No. 914 was moved from the Central to the Eastern section. (AC)

Right:
No. 938 *St Olave's* south of Grove Park on the 14.25 Charing Cross to Hastings, 3 August 1938. (RAS/OJM)

through services from north of London over the Brighton main line and from the Western section by the coast line. The class also worked over the non-electrified lines from Brighton to London via Uckfield, Sussex, also on services from Redhill, Surrey, to Reading, Berkshire.

WESTERN SECTION

The Western section of the Southern Railway, the old London & South Western Railway (L&SWR), had allocations of 'Schools' class locomotives in three distinct phases. The first phase involved the main line from Waterloo to Portsmouth, Hampshire via Guildford, Surrey. The running shed for Portsmouth (Fratton), was a roundhouse with a 50ft (15.24m) turntable and could not accommodate 4-6-0s.

There were triangles at Fratton or at Farlington, where the line out of Portsmouth branched east or west. Nos. 924 to 929 were allotted new to Fratton in 1934 followed by Nos. 930 to 933 in 1935. The locomotives were used to work the express services to Waterloo but axle loading precluded the class from the Central section's mid-Sussex route to Victoria via Horsham.

Electrification of the Waterloo - Portsmouth line in 1936 saw the transfer of the Fratton shed 'Schools' to Bournemouth, another shed with a 50ft (15.24m) turntable, although a 65ft (19.8m) type was installed in the period 1936 to 1938. Most trains starting or terminating at Bournemouth used the West station, and could turn on the triangle at Branksome on the way to or from the shed. The 'Schools'

Above:
No. 915 *Brighton* at Charing Cross on the 11.15 to Dover and Deal, 14 July 1937. No. 915 retains the original chimney, with no capuchon. Loading gauge restrictions have been eased since 1930 and most of the train consists of Restriction 4 carriages. (RAS/JPW)

Left:
No. 937 *Epsom,* in Bulleid-style livery, leaving West St Leonards with a Hastings to Charing Cross train, 18 July 1939. No. 937 is fitted with Bulleid cylinders, a Lemaître exhaust and an extended smokebox. (RAS/JPW)

worked expresses to Waterloo and, during periods when the GWR accepted the high axle load of the class, to Weymouth, Dorset and to Oxford via Reading. During the war years, increased train weights on the Bournemouth line became too much for the 'Schools' and some were replaced by 'Lord Nelsons', no longer required for non-existent Dover Boat Trains. By 1949, the last of the class had left the Western section, although 'Schools' still came regularly to Eastleigh Works for overhaul and were liable to appear on trains either during transfer to and from works, or on trials.

The third phase of 'Schools' activity on the Western section occurred after the electrification of the main lines in Kent. Locomotives transferred to the Western section were based at Nine Elms, London, also at Basingstoke and

Guildford, the latter another roundhouse with a 54ft (16.46m) turntable. Most of their work was on stopping, semi-fast or parcels trains on the lines from Waterloo to Bournemouth and to Salisbury and Yeovil, with occasional visits to Weymouth or Exeter. The class was regularly used on the summer saturday Waterloo to Lymington trains, which they worked to Brockenhurst, and could be turned on the 50ft (15.24m) turntable. The Guildford-based 'Schools' were used with those from Redhill on the Reading-Redhill line.

The last year during which any of Maunsell's express locomotives ran in service was 1962. Bulleid Pacifics and British Railways Standard class 4-6-0s were able to deal with all regular locomotive-hauled passenger services and the D 65xx Type 3 diesel-electric locomotives (later

Right:
No. 901 *Winchester* at Sevenoaks on a down Hastings train in June 1942. No. 901 received a Lemaître exhaust and Malachite Green livery in October 1940. It has a blackout screen on the front of the tender but the cabside windows have not yet been plated over. (RAS/AWC)

Right:
No. 918 *Hurstpierpoint* passing under the Canterbury and Whitstable branch on an up Ramsgate to Victoria express circa 1947. No. 918 was fitted with a Lemaître exhaust in 1940. It was repainted in post-war Malachite Green livery in August 1946. The superheater snifting valves were also removed. (IA/PRW)

Right:
No. 914 *Eastbourne* passing Folkestone Junction on a Dover to Charing Cross train in 1948. The locomotive has a Lemaître exhaust and no snifting valves. *Eastbourne* was one of three 'Schools' to be re-numbered with an s-prefix on Malachite Green livery. (RKB)

Left:
No. 30907 *Dulwich* coming off Hungerford Bridge on the 15.25 Charing Cross to Wadhurst in 1951. No. 30907 is painted Malachite Green with Gill Sans lettering. The Restriction 0 carriages are in BR Carmine and Cream livery. (RKB/ACC)

Left:
No. 30924 *Haileybury* in Folkestone Warren on a Charing Cross to Dover train in 1949. No. 30924 has received a British Railways number on Southern Railway green livery. The first three carriages are Bulleid designed, ordered by the Southern Railway from the Birmingham Railway Carriage & Wagon Co. but not delivered until after the formation of British Railways. (IA/ERW)

Left:
No. 30938 *St Olave's* passing Teynham on the down 'Kentish Belle' in the late 1950s. This all-Pullman train, from Victoria to Ramsgate, was introduced as the 'Thanet Belle' in May 1948. Renamed 'Kentish Belle' in 1951 it ran until the first stage of the Kent coast electrification in 1959. The third rail is already in position. (IA/PRW)

Right:
No. 30931 *King's Wimbledon* passing Bickley on the 14.35 Victoria to Ramsgate, 22 September 1956. The train consists of British Railways-built Bulleid carriages in green livery. (IA/RCR)

Right:
No. 30924 *Haileybury* near Tonbridge on a Hastings to Charing Cross train in the 1950s. No. 30924 is in BR lined black livery with BR Carmine and Cream Restriction 0 carriages. (IA/ET)

Class 33) headed increasing numbers of passenger trains in the summer, when steam heating was not required. Many of the 25 'Schools' which lasted into 1962 saw little service during the year and the last 17 were withdrawn at the end of the year.

The following shed allocations for the 'Schools' class are taken from the late Don Bradley's *Locomotives of the Southern Railway, Part 1* for years up to 1945 and from Ian Allan shedbooks for the years from 1950.

Locomotive	1933	1935	1945	1950	1955	1960
No. 900	Ramsgate	St. Leonards	St. Leonards	St. Leonards	St. Leonards	Brighton
No. 901	Ramsgate	St. Leonards	St. Leonards	St. Leonards	St. Leonards	Brighton
No. 902	Ramsgate	St. Leonards	St. Leonards	St. Leonards	St. Leonards	Brighton
No. 903	St. Leonards	St. Leonards	St. Leonards	St. Leonards	St. Leonards	Guildford
No. 904	St. Leonards	St. Leonards	St. Leonards	St. Leonards	St. Leonards	Basingstoke
No. 905	St. Leonards	St. Leonards	St. Leonards	St. Leonards	St. Leonards	Basingstoke
No. 906	St. Leonards	St. Leonards	St. Leonards	St. Leonards	St. Leonards	Guildford

Left:
No. 30914 *Eastbourne* in BR lined black approaching St Mary Cray on a Victoria to Ramsgate train in May 1957. The eight-car set 473 consists of British Railways Mk 1 and Bulleid carriages in BR Carmine and Cream with a buffet car in green livery. (IA/ARB)

Left:
No. 30909 *St Paul's* approaching West St Leonards on a Charing Cross to Hastings train, 8 September 1951. No. 30909 is painted black and the train consists of three three-car sets of Restriction 0 stock in BR Carmine and Cream. (IA/AAS)

Locomotive	1933	1935	1945	1950	1955	1960
No. 907	St. Leonards	St. Leonards	St. Leonards	St. Leonards	St. Leonards	Nine Elms
No. 908	St. Leonards	St. Leonards	St. Leonards	Ramsgate	St. Leonards	Basingstoke
No. 909	St. Leonards	St. Leonards	Ramsgate	St. Leonards	St. Leonards	Guildford
No. 910	Ramsgate	St. Leonards	Ramsgate	St. Leonards	St. Leonards	Nine Elms
No. 911	Ramsgate	St. Leonards	Ramsgate	Ramsgate	Ramsgate	Nine Elms
No. 912	Ramsgate	Ramsgate	Ramsgate	Ramsgate	Ramsgate	Nine Elms
No. 913	Eastbourne	Ramsgate	Ramsgate	Ramsgate	Ramsgate	Nine Elms
No.914	Eastbourne	Ramsgate	Ramsgate	Ramsgate	Ramsgate	Redhill
No. 915	Eastbourne	Ramsgate	Ramsgate	Ramsgate	Stewarts Lane	Redhill
No. 916	Eastbourne	Ramsgate	Ramsgate	Ramsgate	Ramsgate	Redhill
No. 917	St. Leonards	Ramsgate	Ramsgate	Ramsgate	Ramsgate	Brighton
No. 918	St. Leonards	Ramsgate	Ramsgate	Ramsgate	Ramsgate	Brighton
No. 919	Ramsgate	Ramsgate	Ramsgate	Bricklayers Arms	Dover	Brighton

Right:
No. 30936 *Cranleigh* leaving Tonbridge on the daily train to Cannon Street via Redhill, summer 1954. The Restriction 1 four-car set 453 is in early Carmine and Cream livery with a wide carmine stripe above the windows. This was short lived as it could not be applied to the later Maunsell carriages with deep corridor windows. (IA/RR)

Right:
No. 30939 *Leatherhead* near Sturry on the Canterbury to Ramsgate line, 19 September 1957. This was the South Eastern Railway's route from London to Ramsgate but became a secondary line when through running via Dover became possible in 1931. (RKB)

Locomotive	1933	1935	1945	1950	1955	1960
No. 920	Ramsgate	Ramsgate	Ramsgate	Bricklayers Arms	Dover	Stewarts Lane
No. 921	Ramsgate	Ramsgate	Ramsgate	Bricklayers Arms	St. Leonards	Stewarts Lane
No. 922	St. Leonards	Ramsgate	Ramsgate	Bricklayers Arms	Ramsgate	Stewarts Lane
No. 923	St. Leonards	Ramsgate	Ramsgate	Bricklayers Arms	Dover	Stewarts Lane
No. 924	Fratton	Fratton*	Dover	Dover	Bricklayers Arms	Bricklayers Arms
No. 925	Fratton	Fratton*	Dover	Dover	Bricklayers Arms	Bricklayers Arms
No. 926	Fratton	Fratton*	Dover	Dover	Bricklayers Arms	Bricklayers Arms
No. 927	Fratton	Fratton*	Dover	Dover	Bricklayers Arms	Bricklayers Arms
No. 928	Fratton	Fratton*	Bournemouth	Bricklayers Arms	Bricklayers Arms	Bricklayers Arms
No. 929	Fratton	Fratton*	Bournemouth	Bricklayers Arms	Bricklayers Arms	Bricklayers Arms

Left:
No. 30900 *Eton* on freight. The headcode and the SER signalbox suggest that the train is on the Reading to Redhill line and is destined for Bricklayer's Arms goods depot. No. 30900 is painted black (under the dirt) and was not painted BR Dark Green. (IA)

Left:
E904 *Lancing* approaching Clapham Junction on a Victoria to Eastbourne express in March 1931. The locomotive is as built with no smoke deflectors and with lamp brackets on the sides of the smokebox, putting the disc right in the driver's line of sight. The train consists of ex-LB&SCR low-roofed non-corridor carriages, which Lancing Works was still building until 1924. There are also two Pullman cars. The Western section's Clapham Junction A signalbox is on the left and overhead structures for the LB&SCR's electrification are on the right. These had been replaced by the third-rail system in 1929. (RAS/GRG)

Locomotive	1935	1945	1950	1955	1960
No. 930	Fratton*	Bournemouth	Bricklayers Arms	Bricklayers Arms	Bricklayers Arms
No. 931	Fratton*	Basingstoke	Bricklayers Arms	Bricklayers Arms	Bricklayers Arms
No. 932	Fratton*	Bricklayers Arms	Bricklayers Arms	Bricklayers Arms	Ashford
No. 933	Fratton*	Bricklayers Arms	Bricklayers Arms	Bricklayers Arms	Ashford
No. 934	Bricklayers Arms	Bricklayers Arms	Bricklayers Arms	Bricklayers Arms	Ashford
No. 935	Bricklayers Arms	Bricklayers Arms	St. Leonards	Bricklayers Arms	Ashford
No. 936	Bricklayers Arms	Bricklayers Arms	Bricklayers Arms	Bricklayers Arms	Ashford
No. 937	Bricklayers Arms	Bricklayers Arms	Bricklayers Arms	Bricklayers Arms	Ashford
No. 938	Bricklayers Arms	Bricklayers Arms	Bricklayers Arms	Bricklayers Arms	Dover
No. 939	Bricklayers Arms	Bricklayers Arms	Bricklayers Arms	Bricklayers Arms	Dover

* Nos. 924 to 933 were transferred to Bournemouth in 1937

Right:
No. 914 *Eastbourne* decorated for Eastbourne Jubilee Week, 15 June 1933. (HCC)

Right:
No. 930 *Radley* leaving Brighton on the 11.00 to Cardiff in 1946. The front part of the train consists of 'Ironclad' carriages, built by the Southern to an LSWR design, with GWR carriages at the rear. The third constituent of the Southern is represented by an ex-SE&CR 'P' class 0-6-0T on Brighton shed. (IA/BKC)

Right:
No. 30906 *Sherborne* approaching Gomshall on the 12.32 Redhill to Reading, 22 September 1962. No. 30906 is in BR Dark Green livery and is fitted with a speedometer and AWS. Note electrification warning signs on the smoke deflectors. (IA/DBC)

Left:
No. 30915 *Brighton* near Balcombe on a Whit Sunday Kidderminster to Brighton special made up of LMS 'Period 3' carriages in maroon. The photograph is undated but probably circa 1959. There is a water treatment yellow spot on the cabside. AWS equipment was fitted to No.30915 in August 1960. (IA/DC)

Left:
No. 30917 *Ardingly* approaching Neasden on a Southern Region special for Wembley in the late 1950s. The train consists of green painted Maunsell Restriction 4 carriages. (IA)

Left:
No. 30928 *Stowe* leaving Edenbridge Town on the 16.48 Victoria to Brighton train, July 1961. The train consists of four-car set 467 of 8ft 6in (2.6m) wide Maunsell carriages. (CR/JWM)

Right:
No. 924 *Haileybury* passing Shalford Junction, south of Guildford, on a Waterloo to Portsmouth express, 24 May 1936. Electrification is not many months away but the rails laid in the 6ft (1.83m) way are not electric third rails but running rails, recently removed from the track on which the train is running. (RSC/HFW)

Right:
No. 931 *Kings Wimbledon* at Waterloo on a Portsmouth express. The lower portions of the smoke deflector plates appear to be lighter than the upper parts, both inside and out. The Author has never seen any reference to this being green; possibly it is an effect caused by cleaning. (AC)

Right:
No. 927 *Clifton*, newly repainted in Malachite Green, at Waterloo on a Bournemouth express in 1938. The three-car set 232, for Weymouth, is one of six sets repainted in Malachite Green to form two 11-car trains. Class 'M7' 0-4-4T No. 40 is waiting for the platform signal with a single passenger brake van for Clapham yard. (RAS/OJM)

Left:
No. 932 *Blundells,* with self-trimming tender, on a Waterloo to Salisbury train between Farnborough and Basingstoke. No. 932 is in black livery. The framework for the blackout curtain is still on the tender. The train consists of two ex-LSWR four-car non-corridor sets, reduced to three cars by the Southern in the late 1930s. Two corridor carriages are added to the tail. (IA/MWE)

Left:
Black liveried No. 929 *Malvern* near Millbrook, west of Southampton, on a Bournemouth to Brighton train in 1948. The blackout curtain frame has been removed and the cabside windows re-glazed. In July 1947 the snifting valves were removed. No. 929 was never repainted into post-war Malachite Green. (IA/FFM)

Left:
No. 30923 *Bradfield* in Southampton Docks on a boat train, July 1953. Not having a return working, a boat train would be a suitable means of getting an over-hauled locomotive to London, for return to Dover shed (74C). Two GWR 'Siphon' bogie vans have been added to the train, probably for passengers' luggage. (IA/GW)

Right:
No. 30911 *Dover* at
Honor Oak Park on
the 17.28 London
Bridge to Reading
train via Redhill,
1 June 1962. Trainset
803 is a five-car set
of Bulleid carriages
but the second
carriage is a BR
Mk 1 CK. (CR)

Right:
No. 30911 *Dover*
passing Woodfidley
crossing, east of
Brockenhurst, on the
13.50 Bournemouth
West to Brighton,
18 July 1953. The
locomotive is black
and the Maunsell
carriages are green.
A large proportion
of the Southern's
locomotive hauled
coaching stock never
carried BR Carmine
and Cream livery.
There is a third route
indicator disc on the
near side of the
smokebox door which
is so dirty that the
train runs the risk
of being mistaken
for a Southamton
boat train and being
diverted to Waterloo
at St Denys.
(IA/RWB)

Left:
No. 30911 *Dover* leaving Farnborough on the 13.24 Waterloo to Salisbury in November 1959. The headcode is carried by lamps, not discs. (CR/GHH)

Left:
No. 30937 *Epsom* passing Worting junction on a down Bournemouth train, 4 August 1962. No. 30937, painted Dark Green (under the dirt), is fitted with a Lemaître exhaust, a speed recorder and also AWS. (CR)

Right:
No. 30915 *Brighton*
arriving at
Bournemouth
Central on the 13.50
Bournemouth West to
Brighton in the late
1950s. No. 30915 was
repainted Dark Green
with a right-hand
facing lion on the
right side of the
tender in April 1957.
The British Railways
Mk 1 carriages are in
Carmine and Cream.
(IA/NB)

Right:
No. 30922 *Malvern*
arriving at Clapham
Junction on empty
stock from Waterloo
in September 1951.
It is probably 'running
in' after an overhaul
at Eastleigh works,
before returning to
shed at Bricklayer's
Arms (73B). (RKB/PW)

Right:
No. 30910 *Merchant
Taylors* leaving
Poole on the
12.40 to Eastleigh via
Bournemouth West
and Ringwood,
3 April 1960.
Although not
officially allowed
over the original
Southampton &
Dorchester main
line between
Brockenhurst and
West Moors, 'Schools'
did occasionally run
on that route.
(IA/CPB)

Left:
No. 30910 *Merchant Taylors* between Brookwood and Farnborough on a Waterloo to Southampton train in 1960. Before the Bournemouth electrification, the third rail was laid on the local lines as far as the bridge over the Ascot to Aldershot line. (IA)

Left:
No. 30902 *Wellington,* fitted with AWS equipment, passing Eastleigh on the 12.00 Waterloo to Lymington, 25 July 1959. No. 30902 will take the train to Brockenhurst. The train then went to Lymington and back behind a lighter locomotive. *Wellington* will be turned on the 50ft (15.24m) turntable, to await the return to Waterloo. (IA/RAP)

Left:
No. 30902 *Wellington* leaving Southampton Central on the 11.43 Lymington Pier to Waterloo train, 25 August 1962. No. 30902 is in Dark Green with a left-facing second totem on the right-hand side of the tender. (IA/MJF)

CHAPTER SEVEN

PRESERVATION

Three 'Schools'-class locomotives are preserved and all are
from the batch which was delivered new to Fratton (Portsmouth)
in 1934. All are fitted with the original type of chimney.

In 1960, the British Transport Commission appointed a committee to recommend which classes of locomotives, then still in service, should be represented for a future museum collection, in addition to those locomotives already preserved. A list of 27 steam locomotive classes was produced and an example of each was retained for what later became the National Railway Museum collection. There were some surprising omissions from the list but the Southern was well represented by eight classes, including a 'Schools' class 4-4-0. During the 1960s, the purchase of locomotives for preservation by private individuals or by groups also began to gather pace. Three 'Schools'-class locomotives are preserved, all three from the batch which went new to Fratton in 1934 and all have the original chimney.

No. 30925 *Cheltenham* was claimed for the national collection and, on withdrawal, returned to its original home in Fratton roundhouse for storage. It was later stored at various locations before going to the National Railway Museum at York in 1977, where it was repainted in post-war Southern Malachite Green. It participated in the Liverpool & Manchester 150th Anniversary parade at Rainhill in May 1980 and has since been on static display at the NRM.

No. 30926 *Repton* was purchased for the Steamtown Museum at Bellows Falls, Vermont in the USA. It was repaired and repainted in Maunsell livery at Eastleigh in 1965 before being shipped to Canada in 1967. In the 1970s, it was working on the Cape Breton Steam Railway in Nova Scotia, Canada, where it was fitted with air brakes, cowcatcher, knuckle couplers, bell and electric headlight. The sides and rear coal bulkhead of the tender were raised to give greater protection to the crew when running tender first. During the 1980s, it was repatriated to the UK and went to the North Yorkshire Moors Railway, where it was restored to BR Dark Green livery. The present NYMR Locomotive Footplate Instructor, Keith Gays, once took nine BR Mark 1 carriages up the 1 in 49 bank between Grosmont and Goathland behind it! It makes regular visits to other railways.

No. 30928 *Stowe* was purchased by Lord Montagu of Beaulieu and was displayed outside his motor museum with three Pullman cars in 1964. Initially still in BR Dark Green, it was later repainted in an inaccurate version of Malachite Green with a representation of Maunsell lettering. It was transferred to the East Somerset Railway in 1973, then in 1980 to the Bluebell Railway, where it was restored to its original Maunsell Dark Green livery. It is one of five locomotives owned by the Maunsell Locomotive Society Ltd.

Above:
No. 925 *Cheltenham*, restored by the National Railway Museum to post-war Southern Malachite Green livery. The speedometer is retained but the AWS has been removed. No. 925 is in the Liverpool & Manchester Railway 150th Anniversary procession at Rainhill, 24 May 1980. (AC)

Right:
No. 928 *Stowe* outside the National Motor Museum at Beaulieu, 5 August 1966. It retains AWS and is painted in a non-authentic combination of Malachite Green with lettering in Maunsell style. As far as the author is aware, 'Schools' never worked the 'Bournemouth Belle' service. (AC)

No. 30926 *Repton* on the Great Central Railway south of Loughborough on the 10.08 Loughborough to Leicester train, 15 September 1991. No. 30926 was restored to BR Dark Green by the North Yorkshire Moors Railway and makes regular visits to other heritage railways. (AC)

NAMES

Following the Southern Railway's policy of
naming express locomotives, the new Maunsell
4-4-0 class was named after Public Schools.

The Southern Railway had initiated a
policy of naming its express locomotives
with the 'King Arthur' class 4-6-0s and
followed it by naming its larger four-cylinder
4-6-0s after naval heroes, the 'Lord Nelson' class.
It was inevitable that the new 4-4-0s would also
carry names. After considering county or town
names, the SR decided to name the new class of
locomotives after public schools.

What is a public school? The Penguin Ency-
clopaedia defines it as a private school, inde-
pendent of the state education system, taking
pupils who may be boarders or day attendees and
charging fees. The origins of the schools are various
but they took on their present form following the
Clarendon 'Public Schools Commission' of 1861.
The formal test is that the headmaster should be
a member of the 'Headmasters' Conference'.

Probably the oldest is St Paul's (No. 909),
founded in 1103 as a school attached to St Paul's
Cathedral, London. In 1509, it was re-founded
by the Dean of St Paul's, John Colet, who had
been left a fortune by his father Sir Henry Colet,
a member of the Mercers Company. The school
is still administered by the Mercers Company
and moved to Hammersmith in 1884, moving
again in 1968.

Winchester College (No. 901) was founded
by William of Wykeham, Bishop of Winchester,
in 1382 and Eton College (No. 900) was
founded in 1440 by King Henry VI, the saintly
but totally ineffectual son of the belligerent
Henry V. Its original foundation consisted of a
collegiate establishment of secular priests,
almshouses and a school for 24 poor and
indigent scholars.

Merchant Taylors school (No. 910) was
founded in 1561 by the Worshipful Company of
Merchant Taylors in the City of London and
moved in 1933 to Moor Park. The theme of
commercial sponsorship is continued by
Haileybury School (No. 924), founded in 1809
as a training school for the East India Company.
Wellington College (No. 902) was founded in
1853 as a national monument to the Duke of
Wellington, for the education of the orphans of
army officers.

Endowments by individuals include Dulwich
College (No. 907), founded in 1619 by Edward
Alleyn, an actor and entrepreneur. Bradfield
College (No. 923) was founded in 1859 by the
squire and rector of the parish, the Rev Thomas
Stevens. Other more recent foundations are
Radley (No. 930), founded in 1848 at the existing
Radley Hall and Stowe, founded in 1923 in the
grounds of the 18th century Stowe Park and thus
only established for seven years when it had a
locomotive named after it.

In the following list, the location of each school is shown by its county and the nearest station, with the railway shown where the school was not on the Southern system. A number of the schools have moved since the 1930s and a number of the stations have closed. The counties shown are those in existence in the 1930s. Three locomotives have changed names, one permanently, the other two temporarily. The headmaster of Uppingham (No. 923) objected to the school's name being used on a locomotive, as he was averse to the

school receiving any publicity, so No. 923 was renamed Bradfield. In March 1939, a state visit to London was planned for the President of France and No. 934 *St Lawrence*, being Bricklayers Arms' most recently overhauled 'School', was prepared for the job. Then someone thought that the French delegation might object to seeing the name of the river passing through Quebec, which Britain had taken from French colonists in 1759. The nameplates were switched with those of No. 908 *Westminster*, the delegation's destination.

Above:
Nameplate of No. 30934 *St.Lawrence* at Basingstoke, 18 August 1962. 'Schools' nameplates varied in length according to the name. On No. 30909 *St.Paul's* and No. 30934 *St.Lawrence*, the 'St.' was as shown. On No. 30938 *St Olave's*, the top of the small 't' was in line with the top of the large letters and there was no full point. The *St.Pauls* plate was a short one but *St Olaves* was the same length as *St.Lawrence*, with the letters more widely spaced. (AC)

Locomotive	Name	County	Nearest Station
No. 900	*Eton*	Berkshire	Windsor & Eton
No. 901	*Winchester*	Hampshire	Winchester
No. 902	*Wellington*	Berkshire	Crowthorne
No. 903	*Charterhouse*	Surrey	Farncombe
No. 904	*Lancing*	Sussex	Shoreham
No. 905	*Tonbridge*	Kent	Tonbridge
No. 906	*Sherborne*	Dorset	Sherborne
No. 907	*Dulwich*	London	North Dulwich
No. 908	*Westminster*	London	Victoria or Waterloo

Above:
Nameplate of No. 30918 *Hurstpierpoint* at Eastleigh, 29 October 1949. This was a long plate. The plates for the two-word names (*Merchant Taylors, Christ's Hospital, King's Wimbledon* and *King's Canterbury*) were the same length. (AEW/SWC)

Locomotive	Name	County	Nearest Station
No. 909	*St. Paul's*	London	Kensington Addison Road (a)
No. 910	*Merchant Taylors*	London	Cannon Street (b)
No. 911	*Dover*	Kent	Dover
No. 912	*Downside*	Somerset	Chilcompton (S&DJR)
No. 913	*Christ's Hospital*	Sussex	Christ's Hospital
No. 914	*Eastbourne*	Sussex	Eastbourne
No. 915	*Brighton*	Sussex	Brighton
No. 916	*Whitgift*	Surrey	South Croydon
No. 917	*Ardingly*	Sussex	Ardingly
No. 918	*Hurstpierpoint*	Sussex	Hassocks
No. 919	*Harrow*	Middlesex	Harrow (LNER and LT)
No. 920	*Rugby*	Warwickshire	Rugby (LMS and LNER)
No. 921	*Shrewsbury*	Shropshire	Shrewsbury (GWR and LMS)
No. 922	*Marlborough*	Wiltshire	Marlborough (GWR)
No. 923	*Uppingham*	Rutland	Uppingham (LMS) (d)

(a) St Paul's School moved south of the Thames in 1968
(b) Merchant Taylors School moved to Moor Park (LT) in 1933
(d) The headmaster of Uppingham School objected to the name of his school being publicised, so it was renamed Bradfield in 1934.

Locomotive	Name	County	Nearest Station
No. 923	*Bradfield*	Berks	Theale (GWR)
No. 926	*Repton*	Derbyshire	Repton & Willington (LMS)
No. 927	*Clifton*	Gloucestershire	Clifton Down (GWR)
No. 928	*Stowe*	Buckinghamshire	Buckingham (LMS)
No. 929	*Malvern*	Worcestershire	Great Malvern (GWR)
No. 930	*Radley*	Berkshire	Radley (GWR)
No. 931	*King's Wimbledon*	Surrey	Wimbledon
No. 932	*Blundells*	Devon	Tiverton (GWR)
No. 933	*King's Canterbury*	Kent	Canterbury
No. 934	*St. Lawrence*	Kent	Ramsgate
No. 935	*Sevenoaks*	Kent	Sevenoaks
No. 936	*Cranleigh*	Surrey	Cranleigh
No. 937	*Epsom*	Surrey	Epsom
No. 938	*St. Olave's*	London	London Bridge
No. 939	*Leatherhead*	Surrey	Leatherhead
No. 924	*Haileybury*	Hertfordshire	Hertford (LNER)
No. 925	*Cheltenham*	Gloucestershire	Cheltenham (GWR and LMS)

Above:
Nameplate of
No. 30911 *Dover* at
Bournemouth West,
29 August 1961.
This was a short
plate. (AEW/SWC)

Above:
Driving wheel
of No. 30918
Hurstpierpoint,
with original
crescent balance
weight. Eastleigh,
19 October 1949.
(AEW/SWC)

Right:
Detail of the sanding
gear on No. 30918
Hurstpierpoint
at Eastleigh,
19 October 1949.
(AEW/SWC)

Number Name	E 900 *Eton*	E 901 *Winchester*	E 902 *Wellington*	E 903 *Charterhouse*
Works Order No.	E378	E378	E378	E378
To Traffic	3/30	3/30	4/30	4/30
Smoke Deflectors	1931-2	3/32	1/32	12/32
E-Prefix Removed	12/31	1/32	11/31	11/31
Speed Recorder	none	none	none	11/38
Bulleid Green (1)	6/40 (e)	10/40 (g)	3/40 (e)	9/41 (g)
Bulleid Green (2)	none	none	/41 (g)	none
Bulleid Black	1/43	12/43	3/43	11/43
Lemaître Exhaust	6/40	10/40	none	none
Bulleid Green	12/46	none	6/46	3/46
BR Number	5/48 (i)	10/48 (k)	1/49 (h)	3/48 (i)
Snifting Valves Removed	4/49	10/48	3/50	1/47
BR Lined Black	10/50	10/48	3/50	5/50
Initial Totem	small	BR lettering	large	small
BR Dark Green	none	6/60	4/59	2/59
Totem	none	second (L)	second (L)	second (L)
Speedometer	1/60	6/60	none	none
AWS	none	6/60	4/59	none
Tender Change	none	none	none	706 in 4/62
Re-balancing noted	none	none	none	none
Withdrawn	2/62	12/62	12/62	12/62
Recorded MIleage	1,032,969	1,057,036	not known	not known

Bulleid Green livery applied 1938 to 1942 and from 1946
(e) Olive Green, black edging, yellow lining, black cylinders, green smoke deflectors
(f) Malachite Green, green edging, yellow lining, black cylinders, green smoke deflectors
(g) Malachite Green, black edging, yellow lining, black cylinders, green smoke deflectors

Bulleid Black livery
The dates shown are the next General (Class A) overhaul date after June 1942.

British Railways livery at re-numbering. All later received lined black with the small first totem.
(h) Malachite Green with SOUTHERN tender lettering.
(i) Malachite Green with BRITISH RAILWAYS in Sunshine lettering. No. 30903 was numbered as 30,903 until March 1949
(k) Lined Black with BRITISH RAILWAYS in Gill Sans lettering

Second totem: (L) left facing on left side of tender

Above: E900 *Eton* on display at Windsor & Eton Riverside on the 28 or 29 March 1930. The bufferbeams carry LSWR-style sans serif numerals. (RAS/BW)

Above: No. 901 *Winchester* at Eastleigh in 1935, with the initial modifications applied to the first 10 'Schools' to bring them to the standard of the second and third batches. (AC)

Above: No. 30902 *Wellington* at Eastleigh, 4 April 1953. In BR Black livery, with the lining enclosing the whole of the tender side. (RKB/WG)

Above: E903 *Charterhouse* at Charing Cross, when new in 1930. From E902, the buffer beam lettering was in yellow serif-style characters (AC)

Number	E 904	E 905	E 906	E 907
Name	*Lancing*	*Tonbridge*	*Sherborne*	*Dulwich*
Works Order No.	E378	E378	E378	E378
To Traffic	5/30	5/30	6/30	7/30
Smoke Deflectors	11/31	3/32	1/32	8/32
E-Prefix Removed	11/31	7/31	1/32	12/31
Speed Recorder	1/39	11/38	4/39	9/39
Bulleid Green	1/40 (g)	11/39 (g)	4/39 (a)	11/40 (g)
Bulleid Black	5/42	10/42	4/42	9/44
Lemaître Exhaust	none	none	none	11/40
Bulleid Green	5/46	12/46	3/46	3/46
BR Number	6/48 (i)	9/49 (l)	12/49 (m)	8/48 (j)
Snifting Valves Removed	2/49	9/49	11/49	6/48
BR Lined Black	1/51	9/49	12/49	1/52
Initial Totem	small	blank	large	small
BR Dark Green	11/58	8/58	5/58	7/56
Totem	second (R)	second (R)	second (R)	first
Speedometer	none	11/60	11/60	12/59
AWS	none	none	5/62	none
Tender Change	none	732 in 8/58	703 in 4/62	none
Re-balancing noted	none	1955	none	none
Withdrawn	7/61	12/61	12/62	9/61
Recorded Mileage	1,027,768	not known	1,046,536	1,001,721

Bulleid Green livery applied 1938 to 1942 and from 1946
(a) Malachite Green, black edging, white lining, green cylinders, black smoke deflectors
(g) Malachite Green, black edging, yellow lining, black cylinders, green smoke deflectors

Bulleid Black livery
The dates shown are the next General (Class A) overhaul date after June 1942.

British Railways livery at re-numbering. All later received lined black with the small first totem.
(i) Malachite Green with BRITISH RAILWAYS in Sunshine lettering
(j) Malachite Green with BRITISH RAILWAYS in Gill Sans lettering
(l) Lined black with no tender lettering
(m)Lined black with first British Railways totem

Second totem: (R) right facing on right side of tender

Above: E904 *Lancing* at Clapham Junction, 25 January 1931 on a Victoria to Eastbourne train with a horse drawn pantechnicon on a road vehicle truck behind the tender. (HCC)

Above: E905 *Tonbridge*, when new in 1930. The tenders attached to E905 to E909 had previously been coupled to 'King Arthur' and 'Lord Nelson' class 4-6-0s. (AC)

Above: No. 30906 *Sherborne* in British Railways lined black, with the large first totem. It received this livery in September 1949. (IA)

Above: No. 30907 *Dulwich* at Nine Elms, 20 June 1959. It is in BR Dark Green livery with the small first British Railways totem. (RKB/LGM)

Number	E908	E909	910	911
Name	*Westminster*	*St. Paul's*	*Merchant Taylors*	*Dover*
Works Order No.	E378	E378	E403	E403
To Traffic	7/30	7/30	12/32	12/32
Smoke Deflectors	7/32	1/32	From new	From new
E-Prefix Removed	9/31	1/32	not carried	not carried
Speed Recorder	12/38	10/39	none	none
Bulleid Green (1)	12/38 (b)	2/41 (g)	8/39 (g)	3/40 (e)
Bulleid Green (2)	8/41 (g)	none	none	12/41 (g)
Bulleid Black	10/44	3/44	11/42	7/44
Lemaître Exhaust	none	2/41	none	none
Bulleid Green	none	6/47	none	4/46
BR Number	3/49 (n)	1/49 (j)	12/48 (l)	8/49 (l)
Snifting Valves Removed	6/49	9/47	12/48	8/49
BR Lined Black	6/49	12/50	12/48	8/49
Initial Totem	blank	small	blank (t)	blank
BR Dark Green	8/56	8/58	8/56	12/58
Totem	first	second (R)	first	second (L)
Speedometer	none	12/60	none	10/60
AWS	6/59	none	6/60	none
Tender Change (1)	none	none	728 in 5/55	739 in 3/55
Tender Change (2)	none	none	none	none
Re-balancing noted	none	none	none	none
Withdrawn	9/61	2/62	11/61	12/62
Recorded Mileage	not known	not known	1,093,658	not known

Bulleid Green Liveries applied between 1938 and 1942 and from 1946
(Bulleid Green livery applied 1938 to 1942 and from 1946
(b) Maunsell Green, black edging, white lining, green cylinders, black smoke deflectors
(e) Olive Green, black edging, yellow lining, black cylinders, green smoke deflectors
(g) Malachite Green, black edging, yellow lining, black cylinders, green smoke deflectors

Bulleid Black livery
The dates shown are the next General (Class A) overhaul date after June 1942.

British Railways livery at re-numbering. All later received lined black with the small first totem.
(j) Malachite Green with BRITISH RAILWAYS in Gill Sans lettering
(l) Lined black with no tender lettering
(n) Unlined black with SOUTHERN tender lettering
(t) No. 30910 had a small totem with full-depth tender lining, applied to the unlettered tender in March 1951

Second totem: (L) left facing (R) right facing

Above: E908 *Westminster* as near as it can get to the school whose name it carries. The location is Charing Cross in 1931. (AC)

Above: No. 30909 *St. Paul's,* 21 November 1951. No. 909 received a Lemaître exhaust in February 1941 and BR lined black livery in December 1950. (IA/JFWP)

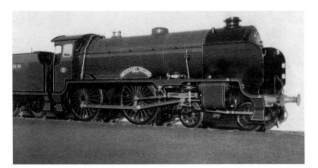

Above: No. 910 *Merchant Taylors,* when new in December 1932. This was the first of the second batch, built with smoke deflector plates and sanding to all the driving wheels. (AC)

Above: No. 30911 *Dover* at Brighton, 13 May 1961. It is in British Railways Dark Green with orange and black lining, with the second British Railways totem. (IA/AGC)

Number	912	913	914	915
Name	*Downside*	*Christ's Hospital*	*Eastbourne*	*Brighton*
Works Order No.	E403	E403	E403	E403
To Traffic	12/32	12/32	12/32	5/33
Speed Recorder	none	none	1/39	none
Bulleid Green (1)	5/39 (c)	6/39 (g)	2/39 (b)	10/40 (g)
Bulleid Green (2)	8/41 (g)	12/41 (g)	12/41 (g)	none
Bulleid Black	7/44	1/45	8/43	7/43
Lemaître Exhaust	none	none	1/39 (u)	10/40
Bulleid Green	5/47	9/48	6/46	none
S Prefix	none	none	3/48 (i)	none
BR Number	3/49 (h)	9/48 (j)	5/50 (m)	2/49 (l)
Snifting Valves Removed	3/49	9/48	3/48	8/47
BR Lined Black	5/50	1/52	5/50	2/49
Totem	small	small	small	blank
BR Dark Green	5/60	6/59	none	4/57
Totem	second (L)	second (L)	none	second (R)
Speedometer	5/60	none	none	8/60
AWS	5/60	6/59	4/59	8/60
Tender Change	1012 in 7/61	736 in 5/54	720 in 8/57	none
Re-balancing noted	1960	none	none	none
Withdrawn	12/62	1/62	7/61	12/62
Recorded Mileage	not known	not known	1,041,595	not known

Bulleid Green livery applied 1938 to 1942 and from 1946
(b) Maunsell Green, black edging, white lining, black cylinders, black smoke deflectors
(c) Olive Green, dark green edging, yellow lining, black cylinders, green smoke deflectors
(g) Malachite Green, black edging, yellow lining, black cylinders, green smoke deflectors
(u) No. 914 had an non-lipped chimney, replaced by a lipped type in July 1943

Bulleid Black livery
The dates shown are the next General (Class A) overhaul date after June 1942.

British Railways livery at re-numbering. All later received lined black with the small first totem.
(h) Malachite Green with SOUTHERN tender lettering
(j) Malachite Green with BRITISH RAILWAYS in Gill Sans lettering
(l) Lined black with no tender lettering. No. 30915 received a small totem on an unlettered tender in June 1950
(m) Lined black with first British Railways totem

Second totem: (L) left facing (R) right facing

Above: No. 30912 *Downside* at Eastleigh, 20 May 1950, In lined BR black livery with the small first British Railways totem. (RKB/WG)

Above: No. 30913 *Christ's Hospital* in Malachite Green with BRITISH RAILWAYS and the cabside number in Gill Sans letters. (AEW/SWC)

Above: s914 *Eastbourne* at Eastleigh, 1948, with a Lemaître exhaust fitted in 1939. It was one of three 'Schools' to receive s prefix numbers in early 1948. (RKB)

Above: No. 915 *Brighton* at Charing Cross on a Hastings train. It was built with a chimney with no capuchon which it retained until fitted with a Lemaître exhaust in 1940. (AC)

Number	916	917	918	919
Name	*Whitgift*	*Ardingly*	*Hurstpierpoint*	*Harrow*
Works Order No.	E403	E403	E403	E403
To Traffic	5/33	5/33	6/33	6/33
Speed Recorder	none	5/39	10/38	10/38
Bulleid Green (1)	12/39 (g)	6/40 (e)	6/40 (e)	5/39 (f)
Bulleid Green (2)	none	none	none	2/41 (g)
Bulleid Black	9/44	1/43	5/43	4/43
Lemaître Exhaust	none	5/40	5/40	2/41
Bulleid Green	none	2/46	9/46	5/46 (o)
BR Number	11/48 (k)	5/48 (i)	10/49 (m)	8/48 (i)
Snifting Valves Removed	11/48	5/48	9/46	12/49
BR Lined Black	11/48	7/52	10/49	12/49
Initial Totem	BR lettering	small	large	large
BR Dark Green	4/58	8/59	5/57	none
Totem	second (R)	second (L)	second (R)	none
Speedometer	12/59	none	none	none
AWS	none	8/59	4/59	none
Tender Change	731 in 2/62	none	none	none
Withdrawn	12/62	11/62	10/61	1/61
Recorded Mileage	not known	not known	not known	1,008,030

Bulleid Green livery applied 1938 to 1942 and from 1946
(e) Olive Green, black edging, yellow lining, black cylinders, green smoke deflectors
(f) Malachite Green, green edging, yellow lining, black cylinders, green smoke deflectors
(g) Malachite Green, black edging, yellow lining, black cylinders, green smoke deflectors
(o) No. 919 had black smoke deflectors

Bulleid Black livery
The dates shown are the next General (Class A) overhaul date after June 1942.

British Railways Livery at re-numbering. All later received lined black with the small first totem.
(i) Malachite green with BRITISH RAILWAYS in Sunshine lettering
(k) Lined black with BRITISH RAILWAYS in Gill Sans lettering
(m)Lined black with first British Railways totem

Second totem: (L) left facing (R) right facing

Above: No. 916 *Whitgift* at Bricklayer's Arms in the 1930s. It still has the original bogie frames and a chimney with no capuchon, which was retained until the 1950s. (AC)

Above: No. 30917 *Ardingly* at Brighton circa 1960. It is in BR Dark Green with the second style BR totem and is fitted with AWS equipment, but no speedometer. (RKB)

Above: No. 30918 *Hurstpierpoint* at Eastleigh, 29 October 1949. It received a Lemaître exhaust in 1940. It is in BR lined Black livery with the large first totem. (AEW/SWC)

Above: No. 919 *Harrow*, as built in June 1933. The V-shape of the lower edge of the bogie frame is clear from this viewpoint. (AC)

Number	920	921	922	923
Name	*Rugby*	*Shrewsbury*	*Marlborough* *Bradfield 8/34*	*Uppingham*
Works Order No.	E403	E403	E403	E403
To Traffic	10/33	10/33	11/33	12/33
Speed Recorder	10/38	4/39	10/39	1/39
Bulleid Green (1)	3/40 (e)	4/39 (a)	10/39 (g)	1/39 (b)
Bulleid Green (2)	none	4/41 (g)	none	10/41 (g)
Bulleid Black	4/42	4/44	1/45	2/44
Lemaître Exhaust	3/40	1/41	none	none
Bulleid Green	8/47	1/48	8/46	7/46
BR Number	10/48 (h)	3/50 (m)	1/49 (l)	10/48 (k)
Snifting Valves Removed	8/47	1/48	1/49	9/48
BR Lined Black	11/49	3/50	1/49	9/48
Initial Totem	large	large	blank	BR lettering
BR Dark Green	9/57	1/59	1/57	12/57
Totem	second (R)	second (L)	first	second (R)
Speedometer	none	none	none	none
AWS	none	10/61	none	none
Tender Change (1)	721 in 9/57	710 in 8/57	724 in 11/52	733 in 3/48
Tender Change (2)	none	1007 in 11/61	none	none
Re-balancing noted	none	none	none	none
Withdrawn	11/61	12/62	11/61	12/62
Recorded Mileage	1,064,713	not known	1,080,316	not known

Bulleid Green livery applied 1938 to 1942 and from 1946
(a) Malachite Green, black edging, white lining, green cylinders, black smoke deflectors
(b) Maunsell Green, black edging, white lining, green cylinders, black smoke deflectors
(e) Olive Green, black edging, yellow lining, black cylinders, green smoke deflectors
(g) Malachite Green, black edging, yellow lining, black cylinders, green smoke deflectors

Bulleid Black livery
The dates shown are the next General (Class A) overhaul date after June 1942.

British Railways livery at re-numbering. All later received lined black with the small first totem.
(h) Malachite Green with SOUTHERN tender lettering
(k) Lined black with BRITISH RAILWAYS in Gill Sans lettering
(l) Lined black with no tender lettering
(m)Lined black with first British Railways totem

Second totem: (L) left facing (R) right facing

Above: No. 920 *Rugby* at Cannon Street, London in the 1930s. (AC)

Above: No. 921 *Shrewsbury* on a Victoria to Ramsgate express composed of the 1924 'Thanet' stock, built for this line before the standard Maunsell carriages appeared. (AC)

Above: No. 922 *Marlborough* approaching Bromley on the 5.15 Ramsgate to Victoria, 16 July 1937. The train is composed of 'Thanet' stock. (HCC)

Above: No. 923 *Bradfield* at New Cross Gate in the late 1930s. In Maunsell green with Bulleid lettering. (IA)

Number	924	925	926	927
Name	*Haileybury*	*Cheltenham*	*Repton*	*Clifton*
Works Order No.	E403	E403	E403	E403
To Traffic	12/33	4/34	5/34	6/34
Speed Recorder	2/39	5/39	11/39	none
Bulleid Green (1)	2/39 (b)	7/38 (a)	8/38 (a)	6/38 (a)
Bulleid Green (2)	9/40 (g)	5/39 (f)	11/39 (g)	2/40 (e)
Bulleid Green (3)	none	5/41 (g)	none	7/41 (g)
Bulleid Black	6/43	3/43	5/44	9/43
Lemaître Exhaust	9/40	none	none	none
Bulleid Green	10/47	12/47	11/46	8/47
BR Number	1/49 (h)	5/50 (m)	4/48 (h)	11/49 (m)
Snifting Valves Removed	10/47	12/47	4/49	11/49
BR Lined Black	10/50	5/50	4/49 (l)	11/49
Initial Totem	small	small	blank	large
BR Dark Green	9/59	1/60	10/60	3/58
Totem	second (L)	second (L)	second (L)	second (R)
Speedometer	none	1/60	10/60	11/59
AWS	none	1/60	10/60	5/60
Tender Change	722 in 11/52	none	none	none
Re-balancing noted	none	none	1949	none
Withdrawn	1/62	12/62	12/62	1/62
Recorded Mileage	1,085,082	1,127,788	1,126,979	1,045,610

Bulleid Green livery applied 1938 to 1942 and from 1946
(a) Malachite Green, black edging, white lining, green cylinders, black smoke deflectors
(b) Maunsell Green, black edging, white lining, green cylinders, black smoke deflectors
(e) Olive Green, black edging, yellow lining, black cylinders, green smoke deflectors
(f) Malachite Green, green edging, yellow lining, black cylinders, green smoke deflectors
(g) Malachite Green, black edging, yellow lining, black cylinders, green smoke deflectors

Bulleid Black livery
The dates shown are the next General (Class A) overhaul date after June 1942.

British Railways livery at re-numbering. All later received lined black with the small first totem.
(h) Malachite Green with SOUTHERN tender lettering
(m)Lined black with first British Railways totem

Second totem: (L) left facing (R) right facing

Above: No. 30924 *Haileybury*, February 1949. It received post-war Malachite Green in October 1947. The BR number and smokebox plate were applied in January 1949. (RKB/PW)

Above: No. 925 *Cheltenham* on a Waterloo to Bournemouth and Swanage express near Hersham in 1938, with a three-coach set of Maunsell carriages leading. (AC)

Above: No. 926 *Repton,* at Bournemouth Central on an up express, was one of seven Bournemouth based 'Schools' to be repainted bright green, in 1938. (DLB)

Above: No. 30927 *Clifton* at Eastleigh, 7 Auaust 1954 painted in BR lined Black livery with the large first totem and large cab numerals. (RKB/WG)

Number	928	929	930	931
Name	*Stowe*	*Malvern*	*Radley*	*King's Wimbledon*
Works Order No.	E403	E403	E496	E496
To Traffic	6/34	7/34	1/35	1/35
Speed Recorder	9/39	6/39	none	11/38
Bulleid Green (1)	7/38 (a)	6/38 (a)	6/38 (a)	7/40 (g)
Bulleid Green (2)	9/39 (g)	6/39 (g)	4/40 (g)	none
Bulleid Black	5/42	1/44	11/42	12/42
Lemaître Exhaust	none	3/41	4/40	7/39
Bulleid Green	6/48	none	7/48	none
BR Number	6/48 (j)	1/49 (l)	7/48 (j)	10/48 (k)
Snifting Valves Removed	6/48	7/47	7/48	2/48
BR Lined Black	12/50	1/49	3/50	10/48
Initial Totem	small	blank	large	BR lettering
BR Dark Green	7/59	12/56	10/56	10/58
Totem	second (L)	first	first	second (R)
Speedometer	none	1/60	4/60	1/60
AWS	7/59	8/61	4/60	none
Tender Change (1)	710 in 5/55	none	none	none
Tender Change (2)	714 in 8/57	none	none	none
Re-balancing noted	none	none	1942	1939 (u)
Withdrawn	11/62	12/62	12/62	9/61
Recorded Mileage	not known	1,138,369	1,096,856	1,057,929

Bulleid Green livery applied 1938 to 1942 and from 1946
(a) Malachite Green, black edging, white lining, green cylinders, black smoke deflectors
(g) Malachite Green, black edging, yellow lining, black cylinders, green smoke deflectors

Bulleid Black livery
The dates shown are the next General (Class A) overhaul date after June 1942.

British Railways livery. All later received lined black with the small first totem.
(j) Malachite Green with BRITISH RAILWAYS in Gill Sans lettering
(k) Lined black with BRITISH RAILWAYS in Gill Sans lettering
(l) Lined black with no tender lettering
(m) Lined black with first British Railways totem
(u) No. 30931 was reverted to original balancing by the 1950s

Second totem: (L) left facing (R) right facing

Above: No. 928 *Stowe* at Waterloo on a Bournemouth express in 1938, finished in the first variant of Malachite Green with large sans serif buffer beam numerals. (RKB)

Above: No. 929 *Malvern* at Eastleigh on an up train, 15 August 1937. The number on the rear of the tender is below the upper footstep. (HCC)

Above: No. 930 *Radley* arriving at Portsmouth Harbour on a Waterloo to Portsmouth express, 22 May 1937. (HCC)

Above: No. 931 *King's Wimbledon* in unlined black in the late 1940s. This was the third 'Schools' to be fitted with the Lemaître exhaust in July 1939. (RKB)

Number	932	933	934	935
Name	*Blundell's*	*Kings Canterbury*	*St. Lawrence*	*Sevenoaks*
Works Order No.	E496	E496	E496	E496
To Traffic	1/35	2/35	3/35	5/35
Speed Recorder	none	12/38	none	none
Streamlined			2/38 - 3/38	
Bulleid Green (1)	7/38 (a)	1/39 (b)	2/39 (b)	5/39 (f)
Bulleid Green (2)	2/40 (g)	5/40 (g)	9/41 (g)	7/41 (g)
Bulleid Black	8/45	10/43	5/45	9/43
Lemaître Exhaust	none	5/40	5/40	none
Bulleid Green	7/48	6/48	1/46	none
S Prefix	none	none	2/48 (i)	none
BR Number	7/48 (j)	6/48 (i)	9/48 (i)	12/48 (l)
Snifting Valves Removed	7/48	6/48	2/48	12/48
BR Lined Black	2/51	12/49	1/50	12/48
Initial Totem	small	large	large	blank (n)
BR Dark Green	none	6/58	2/60	12/56
Totem	none	second (R)	second (L)	first
Speedometer	none	none	2/60	5/60
AWS	none	none	5/62	6/59
Tender Change (1)	705 in 8/58	723 in 3/48	none	none
Tender Change (2)	none	713	none	none
Re-balancing noted	1939 (u)	1947	1941	none
Withdrawn	1/61	11/61	12/62	12/62
Recorded Mileage	1,038,008	1,003,587	not known	not known

Bulleid Green livery applied 1938 to 1942 and from 1946
(a) Malachite Green, black edging, white lining, green cylinders, black smoke deflectors
(b) Maunsell Green, black edging, white lining, black cylinders, black smoke deflectors
(f) Malachite Green, green edging, yellow lining, black cylinders, green smoke deflectors
(g) Malachite Green, black edging, yellow lining, black cylinders, green smoke deflectors

Bulleid Black livery
The dates shown are the next General (Class A) overhaul date after June 1942.

British Railways livery at re-numbering. All later received lined black with the small first totem.
(i)   Malachite Green with BRITISH RAILWAYS in Sunshine lettering
(j)   Malachite Green with BRITISH RAILWAYS in Gill Sans lettering
(l)   Lined black with no tender lettering
(m) Lined black with first British Railways totem
(n) No. 30935 initially had an unlettered tender, then received a large totem in January 1950 and a small type in September 1952
(u) No. 30932 had reverted to original balancing by the 1950s
Second totem: (L) left facing (R) right facing

Above: No. 932 *Blundells,* at Nine Elms in 1939, which ran with a normal 'Schools' tender until 1938 when the tender was fitted with a self-trimming bunker. (RAS/CRLC)

Above: No. 933 *King's Canterbury* at Guildford on the 11.23 Waterloo to Portsmouth and Southsea stopping train in April 1937. (AC/RFB)

Above: No. 934 *St Lawrence*, with green painted footsteps taking St Lawrence boys back to school after the Christmas holiday, 28 January 1946. (AC)

Above: No. 30935 *Sevenoaks* at Ashford, 15 August 1959. It is in BR Dark Green with the large second BR totem and has just been fitted with AWS. (IA/GW)

Number	936	937	938	939
Name	*Cranleigh*	*Epsom*	*St. Olave's*	*Leatherhead*
Works Order No.	E496	E496	E496	E496
To Traffic	6/35	7/35	7/35	8/35
Speed Recorder	none	none	none	8/38 (n)
Bulleid Cylinders	none	5/39 - 3/41	none	none
Bulleid Green (1)	7/39 (g)	4/37 (d)	3/39 (a)	8/40 (g)
Bulleid Green (2)	10/41 (g)	3/41 (g)	11/41 (g)	none
Bulleid Black	11/42	12/45	1/44	3/43
Lemaître Exhaust	none	4/39 (o)	6/40	8/40
Bulleid Green	9/46	9/48	3/46	4/48
S Prefix	none	none	2/48 (i)	none
BR Number	7/48 (h)	9/48 (j)	3/49 (l)	4/48 (i)
Snifting Valves Removed	7/48	12/47	3/49	6/47
BR Lined Black	3/49	1/51	3/49	10/50
Initial Totem	blank	small	blank	small
BR Dark Green	11/59	1/57	10/56	3/57
Totem	second (L)	first	first	first
Speedometer	11/59	9/60	3/60	none
AWS	11/59	9/60	none	10/59
Tender Change (1)	713 in 4/54	738 in 9/61	none	711 in 3/55
Tender Change (2)	723 11/57	none	none	none
Withdrawn	12/62	12/62	7/61	6/61
Recorded Mileage	not known	not known	956,550	998,980

Bulleid GreenlLivery applied 1938 to 1942 and from 1946
(b) Maunsell Green, black edging, white lining, green cylinders, black smoke deflectors
(d) Malachite Green, black edging, white lining, black cylinders, green smoke deflectors
(g) Malachite Green, black edging, yellow lining, black cylinders, green smoke deflectors
(n) No. 939 carried a Stone Deuta Speedometer briefly from August 1938
(o) No. 937 had an non-lipped chimney, replaced by a lipped type in March 1941

Bulleid Black livery
The dates shown are the next General (Class A) overhaul date after June 1942.

British Railways livery at re-numbering. All later received lined black with the small first totem.
(h) Malachite Green with SOUTHERN tender lettering
(i) Malachite Green with BRITISH RAILWAYS in Sunshine lettering
(j) Malachite Green with BRITISH RAILWAYS in Gill Sans lettering
(l) Lined black with no tender lettering
Second totem: (L) left facing (R) right facing

Above: No. 936 *Cranleigh* when new at Eastleigh, June 1935. The edge of the sheet suspended behind the locomotive is visible on the left. (RAS/OJM)

Above: No. 937 *Epsom* at Nine Elms, 11 June 1939. This was the second 'Schools' to be fitted with a Lemaître exhaust and also received new Bulleid cylinders. (RKB)

Above: No. 938 *St Olaves* on a Victoria to Ramsgate train in the late 1930s. Most of the train is 8ft 6in (2.16m) wide stock. (AC)

Above: No. 30939 *Leatherhead* at Eastleigh, 27 September 1952. Painted in BR lined Black with a small first totem on the tender and large cab numerals. (RKB/EWF)

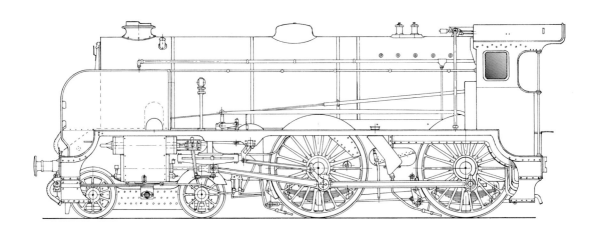

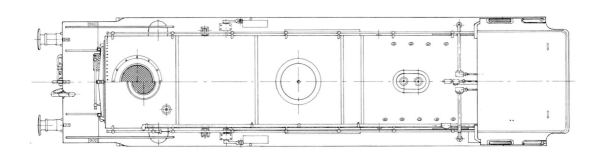

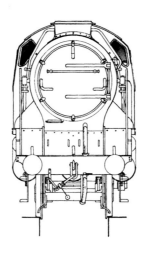

'Schools' class 4-4-0

© Copyright 2006 *Railway Modeller*/Ian Beattie

Above: Detail of the fireman's side of the cab of No. 30911 *Dover* at Bournemouth West, 29 August 1961. (AEW/SWC)

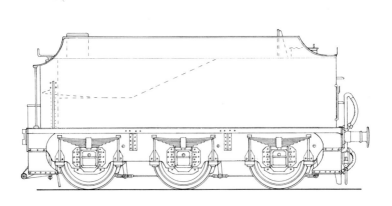

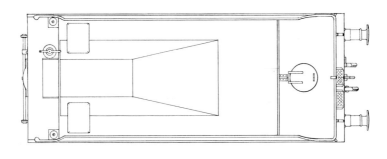

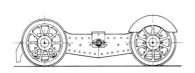

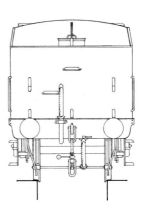

'Schools' class 4-4-0

© Copyright 2006 *Railway Modeller*/Ian Beattie